Reading Fusion 3

Andrew E. Bennett

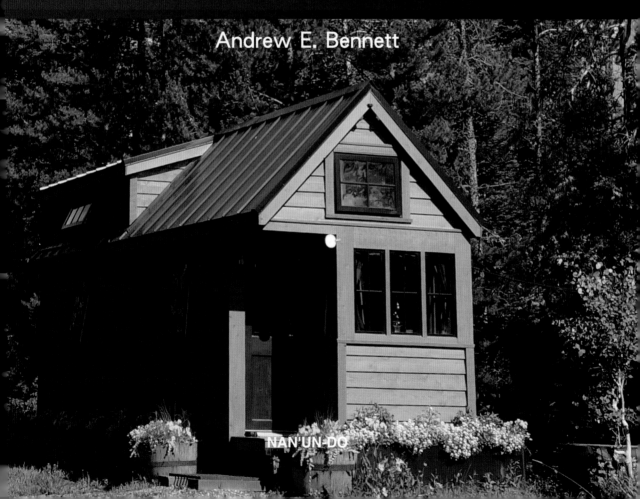

NAN'UN-DO

Reading Fusion 3

Andrew E. Bennett

このテキストの音声を無料で視聴（ストリーミング）・ダウンロードできます。自習用音声としてご活用ください。
以下のサイトにアクセスしてテキスト番号で検索してください。

https://nanun-do.com　テキスト番号 [512038]

※ 無線 LAN（WiFi）に接続してのご利用を推奨いたします。

※ 音声ダウンロードは Zip ファイルでの提供になります。
お使いの機器によっては別途ソフトウェア（アプリケーション）の導入が必要となります。

※ Reading Fusion 3 音声ダウンロードページは
以下の QR コードからもご利用になれます。

Written and designed by: Andrew E. Bennett

Image Credits:
Front Cover: ©Shutterstock.com
Book: All images ©Shutterstock.com, except:
p.10 ©Ray Tang/Shutterstock
p.42 ©A_Lesik / Shutterstock.com
p.72 © MikeDotta / Shutterstock.com
p.80 © Sunshine Seeds / Shutterstock.com
p.82 © singh_lens / Shutterstock.com

Contents

Introduction

Reading Fusion is a three-level series designed to help students improve all their English skills. Each book contains 15 units which center on informative, thought-provoking articles about topics of current interest. A variety of important themes are covered, including the environment, health, technology, arts and entertainment, and many more.

Each unit's main reading passage is 500 words long in *Reading Fusion 1*, 600 words long in *Reading Fusion 2*, and 700 words long in *Reading Fusion 3*. Units open with a series of pre-reading, warm-up activities. Part 1 of the unit consists of reading and vocabulary skill-building exercises. Part 2 contains word-part and grammar exercises, as well as a set of listening and reading practice tests.

The following is a page-by-page visual introduction to *Reading Fusion 3*.

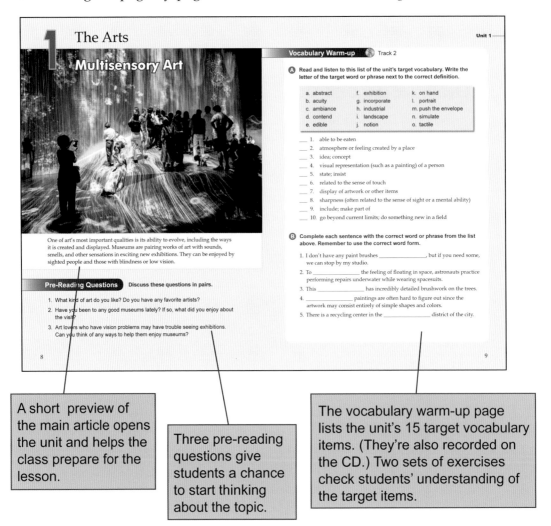

A short preview of the main article opens the unit and helps the class prepare for the lesson.

Three pre-reading questions give students a chance to start thinking about the topic.

The vocabulary warm-up page lists the unit's 15 target vocabulary items. (They're also recorded on the CD.) Two sets of exercises check students' understanding of the target items.

Each reading passage is 700 words long. The unit's 15 target vocabulary items are indicated in bold.

Line numbers to the left of the reading passage provide easy reference.

The reading passage is recorded on the CD.

Part 1: Reading and Vocabulary Building

Reading Passage 🎧 Track 3

When a painting or sculpture is created, the process is dynamic, with the artist breathing in the workshop smells, listening to street sounds, and feeling the materials that go into the work. However, by the time a piece enters a museum, it becomes an object to be seen and not touched. The traditional
5 **notion** that museum experiences should be entirely visual is being upended by multisensory art installations. They **incorporate** the senses of touch, smell, hearing, and sometimes even taste.

One way to make art multisensory is by adding new display elements to existing pieces. For its Soundscapes **exhibition**, the National Gallery in London
10 invited composers and sound artists to write music to accompany artworks. While viewing Cezanne's *Bathers*, art lovers listened to a composition by Oscar-winner Gabriel Yared. Jamie xx, a DJ, created pulsating electronic music to reflect the painting technique and light patterns of *Coastal Scenes* by Théo van Rysselberghe. Sound has the power to trigger emotions and memories, and the
15 exhibition encouraged art appreciation from a new perspective.

The Tate Sensorium display, featuring works from Tate Britain, took matters to another level. The senses of hearing, smell, touch, and taste were stimulated during viewings of four **abstract**
20 paintings. Near John Latham's *Full Stop*, there was a waist-high device that you placed your hand in. Waves of ultrasound **simulated** puffs of air, creating the sensation of rainfall beneath one's fingers. Hand-made chocolates were offered to
25 viewers of Francis Bacon's *Figure in a Landscape*, with ingredients meant to evoke the mood and **ambiance** of the painting. The critical response to the exhibition was mixed, with purists **contending** that masterpieces should stand on their own, and others welcoming the fresh approach.

A visitor enjoys John Latham's Full Stop at the Tate Sensorium.

Entirely new works of art that transcend individual senses are also being
30 produced. The Center of Multisensory Art in Malmö, Sweden, features innovative works such as 3D objects based on photographs. Workshops are also held to discuss new frontiers in art. Another space **pushing the envelope** is the Mori Digital Art Museum in Tokyo, which has 470 projectors and 520 computers. The displays, featuring vibrant colors, touch-activated panels, and
35 more, change as you walk through them, making the experience unique and personal. A turn on the Multi Jumping Universe trampoline creates planets

10

Unit 1

and black holes around you. Children contribute to the exhibition by having their drawings digitally scanned and added to the Sketch Aquarium. And, while enjoying tea at the museum's En Tea House, you can marvel at visual
40 effects projected into your cup.

When it comes to a complete sensory experience, there's nothing quite like the Museum of Food and Drink. You don't just experience displays – you touch, smell, and eat them. The Brooklyn, New York, museum focuses on the importance of food in our lives and cultures. It contains a "smell synth"
45 that lets you mix 19 scents – including popcorn, cinnamon, and nail polish remover – and then smell your creation. For the exhibition "Chow: Making the Chinese American Restaurant," a chef prepared **edible** samples. On top of that, the museum had an **industrial** fortune cookie machine **on hand**. Making the experience more immersive, visitors wrote fortunes which were inserted
50 into the snacks.

Another positive aspect of multisensory art is its ability to make art inclusive for the estimated 285 million people with low vision or blindness. For the Multisensory Met project at the world-class New York institution, clay, nails, and other materials were used to make a touchable replica of an African
55 sculpture. Scents similar to the original object's were added, and electronics inside the replica buzzed when it was touched. A Material Book was made for another sculpture. It let the handler feel the types of materials that went into the piece, with feathers, wood, and porcupine quills providing a scintillating **tactile** experience.

60 Going a step further, installations are being created specifically for those with low vision. Artist Andrew Myers inserts screws at different heights into boards, resulting in touchable **portraits**. And, 3D Photoworks makes 3D representations of famous paintings like the *Mona Lisa*, with touch-activated sensors triggering audio descriptions. As these efforts show, the
65 art world thrives on overcoming limitations and stretching our experiences. Multisensory art has the power to add new dimensions to museum visits, regardless of your age or visual **acuity**.

---

5 upend – turn over; challenge   6 installation – art exhibition   12 pulsating – regularly beating   22 puff – small burst   26 evoke – bring out   27 purist – someone who favors the original creation or traditional style   29 transcend – go beyond   31 innovative – original and creative   34 vibrant – bold and exciting   36 trampoline – platform that you bounce up and down on   51 inclusive – welcoming to everyone   53 Met – Metropolitan Museum of Art   58 quill – pointy spine sticking out of an animal   58 scintillating – very exciting and impressive   66 dimension – level; angle

11

A caption beneath each image shows its relevance to the article.

Beneath the reading passage is a glossary with easy-to-read definitions. To the left of each glossary item is the line number where the word or phrase can be found in the article.

Introduction

Following the passage are five reading-comprehension questions, including main-idea, detail, vocabulary, and analysis questions.

These vocabulary exercises check students' knowledge of the unit's 15 target vocabulary items. There are three types of exercises: synonym, fill-in-the-blank, and word form.

These three questions are also based on the reading passage. Answers should be one sentence long.

Reading Comprehension — Choose the best answer to each question.

...... Main Idea

1. (　) What is the main idea of the reading?
   A. Art that appeals to senses besides sight can be dynamic and inclusive.
   B. Changing the art world requires the support of famous artists and galleries.
   C. Multisensory art exhibitions are mainly put on by British museums.
   D. Supporters of multisensory art believe every artwork should be touchable.

...... Detail

2. (　) Which painting's multisensory display made it feel like water was touching your hand?
   A. Coastal Scenes   B. Figure in a Landscape
   C. Full Stop   D. Bathers

...... Vocabulary

3. (　) In line 54, what does "replica" mean?
   A. sense   B. material
   C. display   D. copy

...... Analysis

4. (　) What is suggested about people with low vision?
   A. Their physical limitations prevent them from understanding art.
   B. Nearly 300 million pieces of art have been created for them.
   C. Touchable objects help them enjoy new and famous artworks.
   D. Every major museum has Material Books which they can feel.

5. (　) What can we infer about the Mori Digital Art Museum?
   A. Because of the changing displays, everyone has a different experience.
   B. Visitors under 16 years old must be accompanied by an adult.
   C. The exhibition incorporates pieces from Malmö and New York.
   D. Jumping on the trampoline triggers a camera which takes your picture.

Short Answers — Write a full-sentence answer to each question.

1. What four senses were stimulated by the Tate Sensorium exhibition?

2. For what purpose are workshops held at the Center of Multisensory Art?

3. How does Andrew Myers create portraits?

Vocabulary Building

A Choose the answer that is a synonym for the word or phrase in italics.

1. At the workshop, experts were *on hand* to provide advice.
   A. referenced   B. available   C. exclusive
2. Monet's *landscapes* are known for their beautiful colors and sense of perspective.
   A. scenic paintings   B. artistic techniques   C. preparatory efforts
3. "Pop-up shops" challenge the *notion* that retail spaces must be permanent.
   A. opinion   B. profit   C. outlet
4. We love the idea of holding the *exhibition* outdoors, but we'll need a backup plan in case the weather turns bad.
   A. show   B. party   C. session
5. The fresh flowers and soft light contribute nicely to the gallery's *ambiance*.
   A. scent   B. mood   C. width

B Complete each sentence below with one of these words or phrases. Remember to use the correct word form.

edible	acuity	tactile	portrait	push the envelope

1. Some children's books add cloth and other fabrics to the pages to provide a(n) _____ experience.
2. The cake looks real, but unfortunately it is not _____.
3. Race car drivers need incredible visual _____ to control their vehicles at high speeds.
4. Filmmakers love to _____ by creating complex characters and plots with unexpected developments.
5. Many countries' coins and bills feature _____ of famous citizens.

C Choose the correct form of the words in parentheses.

1. Some artists (contention / contend) that children create the purist works of art.
2. Flight (simulators / simulates) are invaluable tools in pilot training programs.
3. (Abstraction / Abstract) ideas are more easily understood when specific examples or details are provided.
4. By (incorporated / incorporating) actual objects from factories into her sculptures, the artist makes the pieces relevant and relatable.
5. The (industrialized / industrially) reinforced platform can support several tons of weight.

12

13

Improving knowledge of word parts is an excellent way to strengthen reading skills. This section presents three word parts (one prefix, one root, and one suffix). They're based on word parts found in the reading passage. A short exercise checks students' knowledge of the material.

This listening comprehension section contains either a short conversation or a short talk. The listening transcript can be found in the Teacher's Manual.

The conversations and short talks are recorded on the CD.

Part 2: Focus Areas

Focus on Language

Word Parts

Study the word parts in the chart below. Then read the pairs of sentences that follow. Decide if the second sentence is true or false.

Word Part	Meaning	Examples
ac-	to; towards	account, acquiesce
-pos-	place; put	position, purpose
-um	related to	aquarium, curriculum

1. The workshop is scheduled to be held in the auditorium.
   People will attend the event in a building designed to hear speeches. (True / False)
2. The special effects designer superimposed a second image over the first one.
   To create the effect, the designer removed an image from the frame. (True / False)
3. The accretion of seaweed on the propeller affected its operation.
   The propeller had problems since seaweed was attached to it. (True / False)

Grammar & Usage   *Verb + Noun + Infinitive*

The structure *verb + noun + infinitive* is useful when a person or group is part of a request, order, or other action. Verbs like "tell, ask, order, want," and "need" are frequently used.

Ex: We need everyone to keep their voices down near the nursery.

Ex: Did you ask the electrician to check the kitchen's wiring?

Put the words in the correct sentence order.

1. (to bring / reminded / their sketchbooks / Ms. Lincoln / her students).

2. (to sing / The singer / asked everyone / together / the last ballad).

3. (put the / want us / headphones on / to / Does the tour guide)?

14

Focus on Testing   Unit 1

Listening Listen to the conversation. Then answer these questions.

Track 4

1. ( ) How did the room with the Picasso artwork make the man feel?
   (A) Surprised (B) Sad
   (C) Fearful (D) Angry

2. ( ) Which aspect of the display did the woman NOT enjoy?
   (A) The perfume smell (B) The painting
   (C) The flashing light (D) The music

3. ( ) What does the man invite the woman to do?
   (A) Travel to Central America (B) Attend an exhibition
   (C) Take a history course (D) Help display some art

Reading Read this passage. Then answer the questions below.

Museums are making great strides in turning their permanent exhibitions into inclusive spaces for art lovers with visual impairments. Headsets with audio commentary facilitate self-guided tours, as do tactile maps of museum layouts and braille explanations of specific pieces. In New York City, staff-led "description tours" are increasingly available at famous museums.

Even more enthralling are "touch tours" that allow visitors, wearing silk gloves, to feel original art or cast replicas. The Whitney Museum, Louvre, Met, and Guggenheim are among the institutions that have led touch tours. Working with museums are groups like Art Beyond Sight which specialize in making exhibitions more accessible to low-sighted visitors.

1. ( ) Which of these means of making museums more inclusive is NOT discussed?
   (A) Special maps (B) Audio recordings
   (C) Evening visits (D) Braille descriptions

2. ( ) Which of the following is true about "touch tours"?
   (A) Visitors can wear any type of glove during tours.
   (B) Some of the artwork may not be original.
   (C) The Louvre has been reluctant to offer such tours.
   (D) They are given by every New York museum.

3. ( ) What would Art Beyond Sight most likely provide?
   (A) Lists of galleries with innovative video exhibits
   (B) Guidelines for helping blind museum visitors enjoy art
   (C) Recommendations for the best paint mixing techniques
   (D) Summaries of medical research on eye diseases

15

This section presents practical grammar structures with the goal of improving communicative grammar skills. First comes a short, simple explanation of the grammar point. That's followed by example sentences. Finally, a short exercise checks students' ability to apply what they've learned.

This section contains either a short reading-comprehension passage (such as an article, e-mail, report, etc.) or a cloze passage.

The Arts

Multisensory Art

One of art's most important qualities is its ability to evolve, including the ways it is created and displayed. Museums are pairing works of art with sounds, smells, and other sensations in exciting new exhibitions. They can be enjoyed by sighted people and those with blindness or low vision.

Pre-Reading Questions   Discuss these questions in pairs.

1. What kind of art do you like? Do you have any favorite artists?

2. Have you been to any good museums lately? If so, what did you enjoy about the visit?

3. Art lovers who have vision problems may have trouble seeing exhibitions. Can you think of any ways to help them enjoy museums?

Vocabulary Warm-up Track 2

A Read and listen to this list of the unit's target vocabulary. Write the letter of the target word or phrase next to the correct definition.

a. abstract	f. exhibition	k. on hand
b. acuity	g. incorporate	l. portrait
c. ambiance	h. industrial	m. push the envelope
d. contend	i. landscape	n. simulate
e. edible	j. notion	o. tactile

___ 1. able to be eaten

___ 2. atmosphere or feeling created by a place

___ 3. idea; concept

___ 4. visual representation (such as a painting) of a person

___ 5. state; insist

___ 6. related to the sense of touch

___ 7. display of artwork or other items

___ 8. sharpness (often related to the sense of sight or a mental ability)

___ 9. include; make part of

___ 10. go beyond current limits; do something new in a field

B Complete each sentence with the correct word or phrase from the list above. Remember to use the correct word form.

1. I don't have any paint brushes _____, but if you need some, we can stop by my studio.

2. To _____ the feeling of floating in space, astronauts practice performing repairs underwater while wearing spacesuits.

3. This _____ has incredibly detailed brushwork on the trees.

4. _____ paintings are often hard to figure out since the artwork may consist entirely of simple shapes and colors.

5. There is a recycling center in the _____ district of the city.

Reading Passage **Track 3**

When a painting or sculpture is created, the process is dynamic, with the artist breathing in the workshop smells, listening to street sounds, and feeling the materials that go into the work. However, by the time a piece enters a museum, it becomes an object to be seen and not touched. The traditional
5 **notion** that museum experiences should be entirely visual is being upended by multisensory art installations. They **incorporate** the senses of touch, smell, hearing, and sometimes even taste.

One way to make art multisensory is by adding new display elements to existing pieces. For its Soundscapes **exhibition**, the National Gallery in London
10 invited composers and sound artists to write music to accompany artworks. While viewing Cezanne's *Bathers*, art lovers listened to a composition by Oscar-winner Gabriel Yared. Jamie xx, a DJ, created pulsating electronic music to reflect the painting technique and light patterns of *Coastal Scenes* by Théo van Rysselberghe. Sound has the power to trigger emotions and memories, and the
15 exhibition encouraged art appreciation from a new perspective.

The Tate Sensorium display, featuring works from Tate Britain, took matters to another level. The senses of hearing, smell, touch, and taste were stimulated during viewings of four **abstract**
20 paintings. Near John Latham's *Full Stop*, there was a waist-high device that you placed your hand in. Waves of ultrasound **simulated** puffs of air, creating the sensation of rainfall beneath one's fingers. Hand-made chocolates were offered to

A visitor enjoys John Latham's Full Stop at the Tate Sensorium.

25 viewers of Francis Bacon's *Figure in a **Landscape***, with ingredients meant to evoke the mood and **ambiance** of the painting. The critical response to the exhibition was mixed, with purists **contending** that masterpieces should stand on their own, and others welcoming the fresh approach.

Entirely new works of art that transcend individual senses are also being
30 produced. The Center of Multisensory Art in Malmö, Sweden, features innovative works such as 3D objects based on photographs. Workshops are also held to discuss new frontiers in art. Another space **pushing the envelope** is the Mori Digital Art Museum in Tokyo, which has 470 projectors and 520 computers. The displays, featuring vibrant colors, touch-activated panels, and
35 more, change as you walk through them, making the experience unique and personal. A turn on the Multi Jumping Universe trampoline creates planets

and black holes around you. Children contribute to the exhibition by having their drawings digitally scanned and added to the Sketch Aquarium. And, while enjoying tea at the museum's En Tea House, you can marvel at visual
40 effects projected into your cup.

When it comes to a complete sensory experience, there's nothing quite like the Museum of Food and Drink. You don't just experience displays – you touch, smell, and eat them. The Brooklyn, New York, museum focuses on the importance of food in our lives and cultures. It contains a "smell synth"
45 that lets you mix 19 scents – including popcorn, cinnamon, and nail polish remover – and then smell your creation. For the exhibition "Chow: Making the Chinese American Restaurant," a chef prepared **edible** samples. On top of that, the museum had an **industrial** fortune cookie machine **on hand**. Making the experience more immersive, visitors wrote fortunes which were inserted
50 into the snacks.

Another positive aspect of multisensory art is its ability to make art inclusive for the estimated 285 million people with low vision or blindness. For the Multisensory Met project at the world-class New York institution, clay, nails, and other materials were used to make a touchable replica of an African
55 sculpture. Scents similar to the original object's were added, and electronics inside the replica buzzed when it was touched. A Material Book was made for another sculpture. It let the handler feel the types of materials that went into the piece, with feathers, wood, and porcupine quills providing a scintillating **tactile** experience.

60 Going a step further, installations are being created specifically for those with low vision. Artist Andrew Myers inserts screws at different heights into boards, resulting in touchable **portraits**. And, 3D Photoworks makes 3D representations of famous paintings like the *Mona Lisa*, with touch-activated sensors triggering audio descriptions. As these efforts show, the
65 art world thrives on overcoming limitations and stretching our experiences. Multisensory art has the power to add new dimensions to museum visits, regardless of your age or visual **acuity**.

---

[5] upend – turn over; challenge   [6] installation – art exhibition   [12] pulsating – regularly beating   [22] puff – small burst   [26] evoke – bring out   [27] purist – someone who favors the original creation or traditional style   [29] transcend – go beyond   [31] innovative – original and creative   [34] vibrant – bold and exciting   [36] trampoline – platform that you bounce up and down on   [51] inclusive – welcoming to everyone   [53] Met – Metropolitan Museum of Art   [58] quill – pointy spine sticking out of an animal   [58] scintillating – very exciting and impressive   [66] dimension – level; angle

.... Main Idea

1. (   ) What is the main idea of the reading?
   A. Art that appeals to senses besides sight can be dynamic and inclusive.
   B. Changing the art world requires the support of famous artists and galleries.
   C. Multisensory art exhibitions are mainly put on by British museums.
   D. Supporters of multisensory art believe every artwork should be touchable.

.... Detail

2. (   ) Which painting's multisensory display made it feel like water was touching your hand?
   A. *Coastal Scenes*
   B. *Figure in a Landscape*
   C. *Full Stop*
   D. *Bathers*

.... Vocabulary

3. (   ) In line 54, what does "replica" mean?
   A. sense
   B. material
   C. display
   D. copy

.... Analysis

4. (   ) What is suggested about people with low vision?
   A. Their physical limitations prevent them from understanding art.
   B. Nearly 300 million pieces of art have been created for them.
   C. Touchable objects help them enjoy new and famous artworks.
   D. Every major museum has Material Books which they can feel.

5. (   ) What can we infer about the Mori Digital Art Museum?
   A. Because of the changing displays, everyone has a different experience.
   B. Visitors under 16 years old must be accompanied by an adult.
   C. The exhibition incorporates pieces from Malmö and New York.
   D. Jumping on the trampoline triggers a camera which takes your picture.

Short Answers   Write a full-sentence answer to each question.

1. What four senses were stimulated by the Tate Sensorium exhibition?

_____

2. For what purpose are workshops held at the Center of Multisensory Art?

_____

3. How does Andrew Myers create portraits?

_____

Vocabulary Building

A **Choose the answer that is a synonym for the word or phrase in italics.**

1. At the workshop, experts were *on hand* to provide advice.
   A. referenced   B. available   C. exclusive

2. Monet's *landscapes* are known for their beautiful colors and sense of perspective.
   A. scenic paintings   B. artistic techniques   C. preparatory efforts

3. "Pop-up shops" challenge the *notion* that retail spaces must be permanent.
   A. opinion   B. profit   C. outlet

4. We love the idea of holding the *exhibition* outdoors, but we'll need a backup plan in case the weather turns bad.
   A. show   B. party   C. session

5. The fresh flowers and soft light contribute nicely to the gallery's *ambiance*.
   A. scent   B. mood   C. width

B **Complete each sentence below with one of these words or phrases. Remember to use the correct word form.**

edible	acuity	tactile	portrait	push the envelope

1. Some children's books add cloth and other fabrics to the pages to provide a(n) _____ experience.

2. The cake looks real, but unfortunately it is not _____.

3. Race car drivers need incredible visual _____ to control their vehicles at high speeds.

4. Filmmakers love to _____ by creating complex characters and plots with unexpected developments.

5. Many countries' coins and bills feature _____ of famous citizens.

C **Choose the correct form of the words in parentheses.**

1. Some artists (contention / contend) that children create the purist works of art.

2. Flight (simulators / simulates) are invaluable tools in pilot training programs.

3. (Abstraction / Abstract) ideas are more easily understood when specific examples or details are provided.

4. By (incorporated / incorporating) actual objects from factories into her sculptures, the artist makes the pieces relevant and relatable.

5. The (industrialized / industrially) reinforced platform can support several tons of weight.

Focus on Language

Word Parts

Study the word parts in the chart below. Then read the pairs of sentences that follow. Decide if the second sentence is true or false.

Word Part	Meaning	Examples
ac-	to; towards	account, acquiesce
-pos-	place; put	position, purpose
-um	related to	aquarium, curriculum

1. The workshop is scheduled to be held in the auditorium.
   People will attend the event in a building designed to hear speeches. (True / False)

2. The special effects designer superimposed a second image over the first one.
   To create the effect, the designer removed an image from the frame. (True / False)

3. The accretion of seaweed on the propeller affected its operation.
   The propeller had problems since seaweed was attached to it. (True / False)

Grammar & Usage   *Verb + Noun + Infinitive*

The structure *verb + noun + infinitive* is useful when a person or group is part of a request, order, or other action. Verbs like "tell, ask, order, want," and "need" are frequently used.

Ex: We <u>need everyone to keep</u> their voices down near the nursery.

Ex: Did you <u>ask the electrician to check</u> the kitchen's wiring?

Put the words in the correct sentence order.

1. (to bring / reminded / their sketchbooks / Ms. Lincoln / her students).

   _____

2. (to sing / The singer / asked everyone / together / the last ballad).

   _____

3. (put the / want us / headphones on / to / Does the tour guide)?

   _____

Listening Listen to the conversation. Then answer these questions.

Track 4

1. ( ) How did the room with the Picasso artwork make the man feel?
    (A) Surprised   (B) Sad
    (C) Fearful   (D) Angry

2. ( ) Which aspect of the display did the woman NOT enjoy?
    (A) The perfume smell   (B) The painting
    (C) The flashing light   (D) The music

3. ( ) What does the man invite the woman to do?
    (A) Travel to Central America   (B) Attend an exhibition
    (C) Take a history course   (D) Help display some art

Reading Read this passage. Then answer the questions below.

Museums are making great strides in turning their permanent exhibitions into inclusive spaces for art lovers with visual impairments. Headsets with audio commentary facilitate self-guided tours, as do tactile maps of museum layouts and braille explanations of specific pieces. In New York City, staff-led "description tours" are increasingly available at famous museums.

Even more enthralling are "touch tours" that allow visitors, wearing silk gloves, to feel original art or cast replicas. The Whitney Museum, Louvre, Met, and Guggenheim are among the institutions that have led touch tours. Working with museums are groups like Art Beyond Sight which specialize in making exhibitions more accessible to low-sighted visitors.

1. ( ) Which of these means of making museums more inclusive is NOT discussed?
    (A) Special maps   (B) Audio recordings
    (C) Evening visits   (D) Braille descriptions

2. ( ) Which of the following is true about "touch tours"?
    (A) Visitors can wear any type of glove during tours.
    (B) Some of the artwork may not be original.
    (C) The Louvre has been reluctant to offer such tours.
    (D) They are given by every New York museum.

3. ( ) What would Art Beyond Sight most likely provide?
    (A) Lists of galleries with innovative video exhibits
    (B) Guidelines for helping blind museum visitors enjoy art
    (C) Recommendations for the best paint mixing techniques
    (D) Summaries of medical research on eye diseases

2 Identity

Personality and Inner Growth

When making new friends, talking with classmates, and working with colleagues, our personalities strongly impact our daily interactions. Many theories exist about how personalities develop. There are also techniques for measuring and modifying this fundamental part of our lives.

Pre-Reading Questions   Discuss these questions in pairs.

1. In your opinion, what are the most important personality characteristics? (ex: friendliness, sense of humor)

2. What are the strongest influences shaping one's personality? For instance, are we born a certain way? Is culture the most important factor? What else?

3. How difficult is it for someone to change his or her personality?

Vocabulary Warm-up Track 5

A Read and listen to this list of the unit's target vocabulary. Write the letter of the target word or phrase next to the correct definition.

a. demeanor	f. ingrained	k. self-perpetuating
b. diagnose	g. obedience	l. subscribe to
c. embolden	h. outwardly	m. trait
d. encompass	i. persistence	n. trustworthy
e. in short supply	j. prompt (adj)	o. variable

___ 1. on time; quick

___ 2. personal characteristic

___ 3. follow; agree with

___ 4. behavior; attitude

___ 5. include; cover

___ 6. honest; reliable

___ 7. determination; diligence

___ 8. give confidence to; encourage

___ 9. changeable factor

___ 10. having a limited quantity

B Complete each sentence with the correct word or phrase from the list above. Remember to use the correct word form.

1. _____, Monica is friendly and sociable, but she considers herself a private person.

2. Phil was _____ with a mild hip strain after his bike accident.

3. If a problem is seen as too big to solve and nothing is done about it, the problem persists in a(n) _____ cycle.

4. Complete _____ is expected at the military academy, where the rules must be followed without question.

5. Waking up at 6:30 is such a(n) _____ habit for my parents that they don't need an alarm clock.

Reading Passage Track 6

Whether we are shy or outgoing, curious or conservative, our personality is an important part of who we are. It shapes many facets of our lives, including the way we view the world and how other people see us. Relationships at home, school, and the workplace are all affected by one's personality. As such, a deeper knowledge of its processes and components is a powerful tool in bettering our lives.

Personality is a broad concept, **encompassing** the way we think, feel, and behave – in short, the totality of our identity. In psychological terms, personality involves the way we interpret an experience, what we think and feel about it, and how we react **outwardly**. **Ingrained** patterns of behavior lead to similar responses to new experiences, resulting in comparable outcomes and creating a **self-perpetuating** cycle. Since individuals generally behave in predictable patterns, personality is considered stable over time. So, for instance, if you consider your neighbors to be **trustworthy**, you are unlikely to expect them to act deceitfully.

How, then, does a person become himself or herself? Numerous schools of thought have tried solving this challenging puzzle. While behaviorists emphasize the importance of one's environment, humanists view free will and personal choice as crucial factors. Biological psychologists, on the other hand, see heredity as a determining force. Many scholars, rather than **subscribe to** any one school, see personality as an

It takes a persistent effort to recognize our flaws and correct them.

interlocking web of **variables** including genetics, the environment, parenting styles, cultural issues, and the workings of the unconscious mind.

When it comes to pinpointing the elements of personality, **trait** theory is popular. It involves the identification of distinct characteristics such as generosity and empathy, which may be abundant or **in short supply** for an individual. Personality psychologists, working to isolate the total number of different traits, have generated lists with as few as three traits to lists with as many as 4,000. In recent years, the Big-Five model has gained widespread acceptance. It suggests we all possess, to varying degrees, these characteristics: extraversion, agreeableness, neuroticism, conscientiousness, and openness to experience. Each trait contains a range of potential components. For example, someone who is **prompt** and responsible would rate highly on the metric of conscientiousness.

From country to country, differences exist in commonly held traits, strengthening the view that culture plays an important role in personality development. Parenting strategies underscore these distinctions. Research has

40 shown that in the US and Mexico, parents are likely to encourage children to pursue self-gratification. In contrast, in Belgium and South Korea, restraint and the delay of gratification are encouraged. In the former set of countries, kids learn to become independent, while in the latter, **obedience** is valued. Rather than a question of "right or wrong," parenting decisions should be

45 viewed in the context of each culture, with desirable values measured by their ability to help the child succeed in life.

Given the biological and social forces we are subjected to, the question arises: to what extent can we modify our personality? Many psychologists feel change is possible if we focus on altering habits and belief systems which

50 underlie dominant traits. If, for example, we regularly find fault with people, we can make an effort to look for things we admire about others. With **persistence**, a more positive **demeanor** can emerge. The essential starting point is a belief that change is possible. One informative research project involved students and the issue of brain development. The students who

55 learned that the brain continuously develops were **emboldened** that they too could become better versions of themselves. This newfound confidence led to an improvement in academic performance.

Various assessment tools exist to measure personality traits, the most famous being the Myers-Briggs Type Indicator, which is taken by two million people

60 yearly in the US. This tool and other more specialized instruments help individuals understand themselves, assist doctors in **diagnosing** personality disorders, and provide valuable information to employers looking for the right person for a position. The corporate world's use of these metrics should come as no surprise, as research and experience show that beyond intelligence, being

65 a successful employee requires persistence, reliability, and interpersonal skills. Individuals can also use these assessments for self-edification. By learning more about our personality, we can continue down the road of self-improvement.

---

2 facet – part   11 comparable – similar   15 deceitfully – dishonestly
17 school of thought – position or theory about an issue   22 determining – deciding; main
28 empathy – concern for others' feelings and situations   33 extraversion – the quality of being outgoing   33 neuroticism – the tendency to have negative traits like anxiety and emotional instability   33 conscientiousness – the tendency to be self-disciplined, responsible, etc.
36 metric – statistic; point of measurement   39 underscore – reinforce
41 self-gratification – fulfilling one's desires   47 subjected to – exposed to
50 underlie – rest beneath; form a basis for   66 self-edification – personal betterment

........**Main Idea**

1. (   ) What is the main idea of the reading?
   A. The Myers-Briggs Type Indicator assesses an individual's personality.
   B. Every person is unique, and so is his or her behavior and way of thinking.
   C. Agreeableness is the most important personality trait in the Big-Five model.
   D. Our personality is complex, but we can learn about and possibly modify it.

........**Detail**

2. (   ) Which school of thought feels genetics plays a central role in personality development?
   A. Personality psychology   B. Behavioral psychology
   C. Biological psychology   D. Humanistic psychology

........**Vocabulary**

3. (   ) In line 48, what does "to what extent" mean?
   A. according to whom   B. by which manner
   C. since when   D. how much

........**Analysis**

4. (   ) What does the article imply about parenting strategies?
   A. The strategies are directly related to a nation's desirable values.
   B. Most countries follow a model similar to the US and Mexico's.
   C. Regardless of the culture, parents should emphasize self-restraint.
   D. A family's economic situation impacts such decision making.

5. (   ) According to the article, what might a person do to become less anxious?
   A. Take an assessment test and wait patiently for improvement.
   B. Spend time with calm people and see if they can change you.
   C. Make a diligent effort to modify habits and ways of thinking.
   D. Unfortunately, very little can be done to alter the condition.

Short Answers Write a full-sentence answer to each question.

1. Why is one's personality considered stable over time?

   _____

2. What are the five characteristics of the Big-Five model?

   _____

3. What does a person need to focus on to change his or her personality?

   _____

Vocabulary Building

A **Choose the answer that is a synonym for the word or phrase in italics.**

1. Do you *subscribe to* the theory that through sheer will and determination, a person can accomplish anything?
    A. believe   B. understand   C. suspect

2. Because their positions are vital to a company, accountants must be *trustworthy*.
    A. reliable   B. calculating   C. profitable

3. Without question, Chika's best *traits* are her curiosity and open-mindedness.
    A. ambitions   B. features   C. inquiries

4. One *variable* we can't control during a camping trip is the weather.
    A. storm   B. scenery   C. element

5. Matt's *demeanor* is fairly reserved, but he is a kind and thoughtful person.
    A. background   B. conduct   C. reputation

B **Complete each sentence below with one of these words or phrases. Remember to use the correct word form.**

> self-perpetuating   encompass   ingrained   outwardly   in short supply

1. My cousin has a deeply _____ habit of waving her hands while speaking. She does it without realizing it.

2. With the project deadline approaching, our manager's patience is _____. He'll be back to his friendly self once we're done.

3. The team we've assembled for the debate tournament _____ our school's best and brightest talent.

4. The building looks run-down _____, but the interior is gorgeous.

5. Mario stays up late, wakes up late, and is then late for work. He keeps doing this in a(n) _____ cycle.

C **Choose the correct form of the words in parentheses.**

1. After receiving the (diagnosed / diagnosis), the patient sought out a second opinion.

2. Jake's first year as a restaurant owner was full of setbacks, but he (persisted / persistently), and eventually the business was successful.

3. A conscientious person, Joe responds to phone messages (promptly / promptness).

4. Children who have trouble sitting still for a few seconds may also have trouble remaining (obedient / obedience) in class.

5. (Embolden / Emboldened) by her victory in the local tournament, Rita decided to participate in the national championship.

Focus on Language

Word Parts

Study the word parts in the chart below. Then read the pairs of sentences that follow. Decide if the second sentence is true or false.

Word Part	Meaning	Examples
em-	make; cause	embed, employ
-serv-	keep safe	observation, reserved
-place	location	displace, marketplace

1. The assessment test empowers people to make life-changing decisions.
   Test takers assume their lives will remain the same. (True / False)

2. Salzburg, the birthplace of Wolfgang Amadeus Mozart, is a lovely city.
   Mozart lived in Salzburg, but he was born elsewhere. (True / False)

3. The purpose of placing the antique in the cabinet was to preserve its condition.
   The item was put in the cabinet to protect it. (True / False)

Grammar & Usage   *Former & Latter*

Former and *latter* are useful in saying more about two people, actions, or things which were just mentioned. *Former* refers to the first thing mentioned, and *latter* refers to the second.

Ex: Freud and Jung are two famous figures in psychology. The <u>former</u> was born in 1856, and the <u>latter</u> was born in 1875.

Ex: Today, we'll cover two theories: humanism and behaviorism. I'll explain the <u>former</u> theory, and my assistant will explain the <u>latter</u>.

Complete each blank with *former* or *latter*.

1. Biology and geology are both fascinating fields. The _____ involves the study of living beings, while the _____ is the study of an area or planet's physical structure.

2. You talked about two issues. I am clear about the first one but not the _____.

3. One candidate interviewed for the position this morning, and another came in this afternoon. The _____ candidate was well prepared, but the latter was not.

Listening Listen to the conversation. Then answer these questions.

Track 7

1. (   ) The man brings up an article that he read. What DOESN'T it mention about the pair of twins?
   (A) Their lifestyles   (B) Their clothing preferences
   (C) Their wives' names   (D) Their habits

2. (   ) What does the man think about the idea that genetics decides our personality?
   (A) He agrees genetics is the sole factor.
   (B) He doesn't have an opinion about it.
   (C) He thinks more research is needed.
   (D) He believes the theory is partly true.

3. (   ) What does the woman think about the idea of changing one's life?
   (A) It's possible to accomplish.   (B) Big changes may take a decade.
   (C) Few people can manage it.   (D) Twins are the most skilled at it.

Reading Read this passage. Then answer the questions below.

Every day, we encounter hundreds of situations, such as taking trains, talking with friends, and shopping at stores. Each one requires split-second decisions impacting the way we process information and react. Experts believe flexibility is needed to maintain a healthy personality. That way, we can react appropriately to each context.

When a person has rigid preconceptions and refuses to tailor his or her behavior to each situation, it can lead to dissatisfaction, frustration, and unhappiness. In extreme cases, the pattern may indicate a personality disorder. One way to increase flexibility is by practicing "mentalization" – the ability to internally reflect upon your behavior and that of others. Such introspection, besides teaching us about ourselves, may also increase our powers of empathy.

1. (   ) What may be an indication of a personality disorder?
   (A) Making decisions in a second or two
   (B) Dealing with hundreds of people daily
   (C) Maintaining inflexibility in every situation
   (D) Matching our behavior to each context

2. (   ) The word "tailor" in line 6 is closest in meaning to:
   (A) adapt   (B) deny   (C) retract   (D) amaze

3. (   ) What does mentalization involve?
   (A) Talking with a specialist   (B) Offering to help others
   (C) Thinking about our actions   (D) Imagining the future

3 Nature and Humanity

The Subterranean World

We spend most our time on the Earth's surface, yet the ground below us is also fascinating. Caves are home to complex ecosystems whose survival is linked to the surface world. Important resources like water, tin, and iron are also found underground.

Pre-Reading Questions   Discuss these questions in pairs.

1. What sorts of things can be found in caves?

2. Have you ever been to an underground store or shopping mall? If so, where was it?

3. What are some commonly mined natural resources, and what are they used for? (ex: coal, which is used for energy)

Vocabulary Warm-up Track 8

A Read and listen to this list of the unit's target vocabulary. Write the letter of the target word or phrase next to the correct definition.

a. a plethora of	f. downside	k. replenish
b. adaptation	g. habitat	l. reveal
c. ancient	h. life span	m. sprawling
d. approximately	i. nutrient	n. subterranean
e. critical	j. originate	o. take advantage of

___ 1. show; make something known

___ 2. spread out; taking up a lot of space

___ 3. the length of time lived

___ 4. problem; negative point

___ 5. underground

___ 6. very old; happening a long time ago

___ 7. fill up again

___ 8. start; come from

___ 9. extremely important

___ 10. about; around

B Complete each sentence with the correct word or phrase from the list above. Remember to use the correct word form.

1. Strawberries are rich in _____ like vitamin C and potassium.

2. A common _____ of animals living in cold climates is the development of thick skin or fur.

3. Currently, three bat species are _____ the cave's stable temperature to have their young there.

4. _____ fish were in the lake. I was amazed by how many I saw.

5. Beetles are found in many types of _____, including those which are humid, dry, warm, or cold.

Reading Passage Track 9

Although we rarely think about the land beneath our feet, the **subterranean** world contains a rich diversity of ecosystems and natural resources. Caves and other underground **habitats** are home to thousands of fish, insect, and animal species, as well as some human cultures. The water and minerals
5 buried in the soil are of **critical** importance to nearly all of us. As such, there's a growing awareness of the need to preserve these special environments and use their resources wisely.

Sinkholes and caves, known as "karst" landscapes, are formed by the slow dissolution of rocks by rain and soil water. Completely lacking in light, these
10 areas rely on **nutrients** which **originate** on the surface. Crickets, salamanders, fish, and beetles are among the creatures that have learned to thrive underground. Their striking **adaptations** include longer **life spans**, a loss of sight, and a highly developed sense of touch. For example, crayfish in Shelta Cave, Alabama, live to 100 years or longer, and they don't start reproducing
15 until they are 35 years old.

Many species of bats spend part of their time in caves, which make ideal maternity and hibernating sites. Colonies can be enormous, such as Bracken Cave in Texas, home to 20 million Mexican free-
20 tailed bats. Yet these ecosystems are fragile. A study of 225 cave systems in China **revealed** that 90% of them were disturbed by people – mostly tourists. Entrances need to be properly gated to protect caves and their inhabitants.

This impressive Cappadocia cave structure has multiple rooms and passageways.

25 For millennia, people have also **taken advantage of** the natural shelter provided by underground spaces. The Cappadocia region in Turkey contains soft rock produced millions of years ago by the slow hardening of volcanic ash. The composition of the material allowed **ancient** civilizations to carve networks of homes, storage spaces, and tunnels into the rock. Derinkuyu, one
30 of the largest underground cities, contains an incredible 11 levels.

In modern times, Montréal, Canada, is home to the **sprawling** underground city known as RÉSO. The 33 km of connected areas are always comfortable, even in the freezing winter. There are almost 1,700 shops and 200 restaurants, as well as hotels, apartments, and universities. Interestingly, many locations
35 are extensions of above-ground structures like skyscrapers, showing the interconnectedness of the surface and subterranean worlds.

Wherever people live, underground resources are essential to our well-being. Groundwater, the most widely used natural resource, is found buried in layers of rock, soil, gravel, and clay. These "aquifers" supply one-half of the world's
40 drinking water while irrigating countless farms. In countries like Bahrain and Malta, 100% of all fresh water comes from aquifers.

These repositories are slowly **replenished** by rain water and melting snow, but the process can take years, and groundwater is often removed faster than it can be replaced. A NASA study of the 37 largest aquifers revealed that 21
45 were in danger of being depleted. A related problem is the sinking of the land above overused sites. Due to groundwater removal, parts of Mexico City are sinking at a rate of 2.5 cm per month. Care needs to be taken to use aquifers responsibly and protect them from pollutants.

The mining industry is based on digging up the treasures beneath us to
50 provide raw materials for **a plethora of** businesses. For example, in the construction industry, sand, gravel, and bauxite are essential materials. Precious metals like gold and silver are important not only for coins and jewelry but also for electronics, scientific equipment, and dentistry. Even Earth-friendly items such as solar panels are only possible because of mining.

55 However, all that digging has its **downsides**. Quarries and mines can devastate ecosystems and pollute water sources. Also, although **approximately** 1% of the world's workforce is in mining, the field is responsible for 8% of all fatal workplace accidents. Furthermore, changes in the global economy can have a dramatic impact on the mining industry,
60 whose market value fell from $1.6 trillion in 2010 to $494 billion in 2017.

The balance between the surface and subterranean worlds is delicate. They are linked in a web of interdependence, and when it is disrupted, the consequences can be severe. We need to make smart decisions when it comes to protecting the soil, karst ecosystems, and aquifers. By using underground
65 resources wisely, we can ensure they will be available for future generations.

---

5 as such – therefore   9 dissolution – dissolving   11 thrive – be very successful
12 striking – impressive   17 hibernate – rest in deep sleep for a long period   25 millennium (plural: millennia) – period of 1,000 years   36 interconnectedness – state of being linked
40 irrigate – provide water to farmlands   42 repository – storage place   44 NASA – American space agency   51 gravel – very small stones   51 bauxite – type of rock used to make aluminum
55 quarry – site from which rocks or other items are mined   56 devastate – destroy

Choose the best answer to each question.

.... **Main Idea**

1. (   ) What is the main idea of the reading?
   A. Karst landscapes are among the most fascinating underground places.
   B. The world below us is important for ecological and economic reasons.
   C. Subterranean ecosystems may be more diverse than surface habitats.
   D. Though expensive, mining precious metals has widespread benefits.

.... **Detail**

2. (   ) How old are Shelta Cave crayfish when they start reproducing?
   A. 20 years old   B. 35 years old
   C. 90 years old   D. 100 years old

.... **Vocabulary**

3. (   ) In line 11, what does "creatures" mean?
   A. living beings   B. karst landscapes
   C. special adaptations   D. natural resources

.... **Analysis**

4. (   ) What does the article suggest about the Cappadocia region?
   A. It's the only place in the world with rock formed by volcanic ash.
   B. It took millions of years for people to build subterranean cities there.
   C. Creating underground structures was made easier by the soft rock.
   D. Derinkuku is the only city there that has multiple levels.

5. (   ) What reason is NOT given for using underground resources wisely?
   A. NASA has reported the 37 largest aquifers will never be depleted.
   B. The overuse of groundwater supplies may cause the land to sink.
   C. Digging up coal and other materials might pollute water sources.
   D. The mining activities at quarries endanger nearby ecosystems.

Short Answers Write a full-sentence answer to each question.

1. How are karst landscapes formed?

_____

2. What are two countries that get all of their fresh water from aquifers?

_____

3. In what ways are precious metals like gold important?

_____

28

Vocabulary Building

A Choose the answer that is a synonym for the word or phrase in italics.

1. These *ancient* rock formations tell us a great deal about local geology.
   A. complex   B. thick   C. very old

2. Investigators believe the fire *originated* near one of the park's campsites.
   A. started   B. damaged   C. blamed

3. A *downside* of the tracking equipment is it is unreliable when temperatures fall to five degrees or lower.
   A. feature   B. problem   C. range

4. The *sprawling* Northeast Greenland National Park covers nearly one million square kilometers.
   A. huge   B. beautiful   C. cold

5. There are *a plethora of* reasons for protecting our oceans and coastal areas.
   A. outstanding   B. unreasonable   C. numerous

B Complete each sentence below with one of these words or phrases. Remember to use the correct word form.

> nutrient   life span   subterranean   habitat   take advantage of

1. Let's _____ the gorgeous weather and go hiking.

2. Fangtooth fish, which occupy very deep _____, have been observed nearly 5,000 meters below the Earth's surface.

3. Because vitamin D is an essential _____, not getting enough of it can lead to health problems.

4. Central Europe's cave salamanders have _____ of up to 58 years.

5. Many_____ organisms are microscopic, living in the gaps between rocks and soil particles.

C Choose the correct form of the words in parentheses.

1. The decline of spider and bat populations is (reveals / revealing) proof of the need to protect the cave.

2. It's (critical / critically) that we give the aquifer enough time to recharge.

3. The surveyor has determined the (approximate / approximately) quantity of zinc in the mine.

4. Shouldn't we (replenish / replenishment) our supplies before continuing the trip?

5. Species that cannot (adapt / adaptation) to a shift in environmental conditions risk going extinct.

Focus on Language

Word Parts

Study the word parts in the chart below. Then read the pairs of sentences that follow. Decide if the second sentence is true or false.

Word Part	Meaning	Examples
eco-	related to the environment	ecology, ecosystem
-civ-	citizen	civilization, uncivil
-ance	related to an action or quality	appearance, significance

1. The growth of farming 14,000 years ago allowed civilizations to develop.

   Farming had a negative impact on the growth of human cultures. (True / False)

2. The reliance of subterranean creatures on food from the surface means they may not survive if the food supply is limited.

   The stability of above-ground food supplies is directly related to the survival of underground life forms. (True / False)

3. Costa Rica welcomes eco-tourists from around the world.

   A special class of visitor travels there to enjoy its natural places. (True / False)

Grammar & Usage   *Even, Even though, & Even so*

Even is an adverb which adds emphasis to a word, clause, or sentence. *Even though* is used in an adverb clause, and it means "although." *Even so* means "although that is true."

Ex: <u>Even</u> small caves may be home to thousands of creatures.

Ex: <u>Even though</u> the bracelet is expensive, Sheila still wants it.

Ex: Digging the well will be difficult. <u>Even so</u>, we have to try.

Complete each sentence with *even*, *even though*, or *even so*.

1. _____ it snowed heavily last winter, the aquifer is nearly dry.

2. _____ microscopic creatures play important roles in their ecosystems.

3. The land is sinking from groundwater overuse. _____, the city doesn't want to reduce the water extraction rate.

Listening   Listen to the short talk. Then answer these questions.

Track 10

1. ( ) What is the purpose of the talk?
   - (A) To encourage investment in a mining project
   - (B) To welcome people on a tour
   - (C) To teach a technique to some art students
   - (D) To announce a new contest

2. ( ) According to the speaker, what has helped preserve the salt carvings?
   - (A) The thickness of the rock   (B) The skill of the miners
   - (C) The donations of the visitors (D) The temperature of the mine

3. ( ) How long did it take to build the Chapel of St. Kinga?
   - (A) 18 years   (B) 30 years
   - (C) 54 years   (D) 300 years

Reading   Read this information. Then answer the questions below.

The theme for this year's Symposium on Sustainable Mining is "Green Prosperity for All." Presentations will focus on the following issues:

1) Many untapped caches of platinum group metals are located in developing countries. When mining them, how can we partner with local government agencies and stake holders to create a win-win situation for all sides?
2) How can we counter the perception that our industry is at odds with environmental protection?
3) Consumers and utility companies enjoy tax incentives for installing solar panels and windmills. As the raw material suppliers for this equipment, should we make the case that we deserve similar tax breaks?
4) How can we lend our expertise to recycling initiatives to boost their efficiency and help integrate recycled materials into the supply chain?

1. ( ) What aspect of mining operations will NOT be covered?
   - (A) Recycling efforts   (B) Management costs
   - (C) Tax considerations   (D) Public opinions

2. ( ) The phrase "at odds with" in line 7 is closest in meaning to:
   - (A) even   (B) undeserved
   - (C) against   (D) perceived

3. ( ) The director of a bauxite mine will discuss his experience consulting for a recycler. What issue does this talk correspond to?
   - (A) Issue 1   (B) Issue 2
   - (C) Issue 3   (D) Issue 4

4

Elements of Genius

Look deep, deep into nature, and then you will understand everything better.

Albert Einstein

JERSEY

£2

$$G_{\mu\nu} = 8\pi T_{\mu\nu}$$

Geniuses like Wolfgang Amadeus Mozart and Albert Einstein have influenced the arts and sciences so profoundly that it's hard to imagine a world without their accomplishments. Although brilliant thinkers, musicians, and artists are all unique, they tend to share certain characteristics.

Pre-Reading Questions   Discuss these questions in pairs.

1. Who are some famous geniuses and what are they known for?

2. What might be some characteristics that geniuses have in common?

3. Is it possible for anyone to be a genius? Why or why not?

Vocabulary Warm-up Track 11

A Read and listen to this list of the unit's target vocabulary. Write the letter of the target word or phrase next to the correct definition.

a. ahead of its time	f. de facto	k. perseverance
b. boundary	g. entail	l. quantify
c. calculation	h. in tandem	m. reject
d. characterize	i. majority	n. surmise
e. concentration	j. meticulous	o. tackle

___ 1. guess

___ 2. assign a numerical value

___ 3. more than 50% of a group

___ 4. limit; edge

___ 5. involve; include

___ 6. the quality of not giving up

___ 7. describe in a certain way

___ 8. together; along with

___ 9. more advanced than what others are doing

___ 10. very careful; paying close attention to detail

B Complete each sentence with the correct word or phrase from the list above. Remember to use the correct word form.

1. Carl is the _____ leader of the group. He doesn't have an official title, but everyone listens to him.

2. The proposal was _____ because it would have been too expensive.

3. During our next meeting, we'll _____ the question of how to pay for a new copy machine.

4. Though the _____ involved several 15-digit numbers, the computer handled it easily.

5. The _____ of so many technology companies in Silicon Valley makes it easy to find experts for difficult computing jobs.

Reading Passage Track 12

Like the brightest stars in the sky, the geniuses among us shine the most brilliantly. The world has reaped incalculable benefits from the music of Ludwig van Beethoven, the astronomy of Galileo Galilei, and the chemistry of Marie Curie, to name a few. What is it that enables a single person to change
5 the course of history? **Characterizing** genius is difficult, but identifying some common elements has helped uncover its secrets.

Geniuses either expand the **boundaries** of existing disciplines or create entirely new ones. Take Isaac Newton. One day in 1666, he watched an apple fall from a tree (which still stands). **Surmising** there must be a force pulling
10 the apple downward, his curiosity drove him to invent calculus and discover the law of gravity, forever changing mathematics and physics. Sadly, such accomplishments are not always recognized by one's peers. The paintings of Vincent van Gogh and poems of Emily Dickinson were only celebrated after their deaths.

15 What, then, are the elements of genius? A high level of intelligence is common, but it's a complex attribute. IQ tests have been the **de facto** standard of measurement since 1920, yet plenty of brilliant people have scored below the top of the curve.
20 In 1921, Lewis Terman of Stanford University began a longitudinal study of children who scored at least 140 on an IQ test. Terman **rejected** Luis Alvarez and William Shockley from the study because of their scores, yet they both went on to win Nobel Prizes.

Dancers perform through their movements, using a special brand of creativity and intelligence.

25 One reason these tests are questionable is that they focus on problem solving through specific abilities like verbal skills and logical reasoning. People who think "outside the box" often use unorthodox, imaginative methods to **tackle** challenges. What's more, Howard Gardner's theory of multiple intelligences suggests there are not one or two but *eight* types of intelligence. They include
30 musical skills, interpersonal know-how, and bodily-kinesthetic intelligence, which involves the use of one's body to learn, as a dancer might. Though **quantifying** such abilities is difficult, this broader framework of intelligence helps us understand how a variety of geniuses can exist.

Another component of genius that we are learning more about is creativity.
35 It **entails** finding the links between diverse concepts and producing original ideas. The works of William Shakespeare, Fyodor Dostoevsky, and other

authors require the ability to envision plots as intricate and meaningful as the writing itself. Theoretical physicists also need vast imaginative powers. Albert Einstein conceived the Special Theory of Relativity through a combination of
40 abstract thought and years of careful **calculations**. So **ahead of its time** was his work that physicists using the latest technology were only able to prove him right a century later.

The act of creating involves different parts of the brain working **in tandem**. One study of genius thinkers found that each of them had a corpus callosum
45 (which facilitates connections between the left and right hemispheres) with an especially high **concentration** of nerve fibers. Their brains were hardwired for rapid analysis and production. In another study, fMRI scans were performed on especially creative people. They had heightened levels of activity in parts of the brain related to auditory, visual, and other types of information
50 processing. This evidence supports those who believe that genetics is an important component of being a genius.

One isn't simply born into greatness, though. History shows us that dedication and **perseverance** are also required. The **majority** of geniuses have followed the "ten-year rule." That is, it took them at least a decade of focused work
55 to generate a masterpiece or make a major breakthrough. Charles Darwin, known for his **meticulous** observations, spent two decades crafting his masterwork *The Origin of Species*. "Accidental" breakthroughs can occur, such as Alexander Fleming's discovery of penicillin. But as the saying goes, Dr. Fleming "made his own luck." He laid the groundwork for his breakthrough
60 through years of experimentation.

Whether one is a performer, musician, writer, or scientist, a combination of attributes goes into being a genius. It also helps to be in the right place at the right time. Leonardo da Vinci, who was an engineer, mathematician, botanist, and more, lived during the Italian Renaissance alongside the likes of
65 Raphael and Michelangelo. In today's world, we are all connected by modern technology. Just imagine what geniuses are yet to emerge and what amazing feats they will accomplish.

---

[2] reap – gather; receive   [2] incalculable – extremely large   [4] to name a few – there are many others   [17] IQ – intelligence quotient   [19] curve – a distribution of data points drawn as a curved line   [21] longitudinal – taking place over a long period of time
[27] unorthodox – unusual   [30] kinesthetic – related to the sensation and awareness of one's movements   [37] envision – see; imagine   [45] facilitate – make possible or easier
[45] hemisphere – half of a sphere (ex: the brain's left hemisphere)   [47] fMRI – functional magnetic resonance imaging   [58] penicillin – type of antibiotic drug   [64] botanist – person who studies plants   [64] Italian Renaissance – a period of great progress in the arts and sciences

Choose the best answer to each question.

.... Main Idea

1. (   ) What is the main idea of the reading?
   A. Geniuses often have similar characteristics helping them achieve greatness.
   B. Leonardo da Vinci was the most creative genius in history.
   C. The 20th century produced more geniuses than any period.
   D. Being a genius in the arts is more difficult than being one in the sciences.

.... Detail

2. (   ) Which genius made a great discovery by chance?
   A. Albert Einstein   B. Fyodor Dostoevsky
   C. Alexander Fleming   D. Emily Dickinson

.... Vocabulary

3. (   ) In line 7, what does "discipline" mean?
   A. punishment   B. authority
   C. control   D. field

.... Analysis

4. (   ) What does the article imply about Luis Alvarez?
   A. He scored less than 140 on an IQ test.
   B. He was more intelligent than William Shockley.
   C. He was a lifelong friend of Lewis Terman.
   D. He attended Stanford University in the 1920s.

5. (   ) What are we most likely to see from an extremely creative thinker?
   A. A high level of interpersonal intelligence but poor musical skills
   B. A corpus callosum with an unusually large number of nerve fibers
   C. A masterpiece made ten months after the person began working
   D. A career spent mostly alone, with little contact with other geniuses

Short Answers **Write a full-sentence answer to each question.**

1. What two fields of study were greatly influenced by Newton's discovery?

_____

2. Why was Einstein's Special Theory of Relativity ahead of its time?

_____

3. How has the "ten-year rule" applied to the majority of geniuses?

_____

Vocabulary Building

A Choose the answer that is a synonym for the word or phrase in italics.

1. This medical dictionary is the *de facto* standard. Everyone uses it.
   A. actual   B. technical   C. giant

2. When a work of art is *ahead of its time*, it may be years before it is widely appreciated.
   A. very advanced   B. too abstract   C. well-liked

3. *Tackling* climate change will require the cooperation of the world's governments.
   A. Ignoring   B. Convincing   C. Handling

4. With your qualifications, I doubt your application will be *rejected*.
   A. considered   B. shared   C. refused

5. Can you please double check my *calculations* to make sure they are accurate?
   A. theories   B. computations   C. colleagues

B Complete each sentence below with one of these words or phrases. Remember to use the correct word form.

majority	quantify	in tandem	boundary	concentration

1. With the supercomputers working _____, the analysis will be completed by this afternoon.

2. The _____ of us agree we should recruit new club members.

3. Why is there a heavy _____ of minerals in these rocks?

4. If I had to _____ the invention's value in terms of the time and resources we'll save, I'd put it at $10 million.

5. This street marks the northernmost _____ of our district.

C Choose the correct form of the words in parentheses.

1. First, the instruments must be (meticulous / meticulously) cleaned.

2. (Surmising / Surmise) the waves would be rough, the captain ordered everything on deck to be strapped down.

3. My mother told me if I (persevere / perseverance), I can overcome any obstacle.

4. The study will (entail / entailing) interviewing subjects from 12 countries.

5. I wouldn't (characterize / characterization) the play as perfect, but it is entertaining.

Focus on Language

Word Parts

Study the word parts in the chart below. Then read the pairs of sentences that follow. Decide if the second sentence is true or false.

Word Part	Meaning	Examples
ab-	away	absent, abundant
-aud-	listen; hear	inaudible, auditorium
-ory	related to	sensory, mandatory

1. Because the formula was so complex, explanatory notes were attached.
   Information was provided to explain the formula. (True / False)

2. The MRI scan revealed something abnormal in her brain's left hemisphere.
   Everything was what you would expect to see in a healthy person. (True / False)

3. There is an audible clicking noise coming from the instrument panel.
   The sound is so faint that most people can't hear it. (True / False)

Grammar & Usage   *Either…or, Neither…nor, & Both…and*

Either…or presents a pair of choices. *Neither…nor* presents two items in a negative state. *Both…and* presents two items in a positive state. For all of these pairs, the two items are both nouns.

Ex: <u>Either</u> Dr. Pendleton <u>or</u> Dr. Chen has the key to the lab.

Ex: <u>Neither</u> the lute <u>nor</u> the harpsichord is widely played anymore.

Ex: <u>Both</u> the Nobel Prize <u>and</u> Pritzker Prize are prestigious awards.

Fill in the blanks with *Either...or, Neither...nor*, or *Both...and*.

1. _____ astrophysics _____ nuclear physics is an easy area of study. Each requires many years of coursework.

2. _____ Euclid _____ Pythagoras were important Greek mathematicians. They made major contributions to the field.

3. _____ water _____ heat caused the damage. Which do you think it was?

Listening Listen to the conversation. Then answer these questions.

Track 13

1. (   ) Where are the people?
   (A) At a music store   (B) At the woman's house
   (C) At a museum   (D) At a concert hall

2. (   ) What does the man imply?
   (A) He was not a talented young musician.
   (B) Mozart wrote beautiful music with little effort.
   (C) The woman is right about the string section.
   (D) Symphonies are his favorite type of music.

3. (   ) Where is the woman getting information about Mozart?
   (A) From a booklet   (B) From an old friend
   (C) From a musician   (D) From an audio recording

Reading Fill in each blank with a word or phrase from each group below.

During Albert Einstein's life, the world marveled at his brilliance. After his death in 1955, Einstein's brain was photographed and studied in an attempt (1) any physical underpinnings for his genius. Several detailed reports have been made. Interestingly, the brain's weight is 1.22 kg, (2) is lighter than the average of 1.36 kg. However, the brain's inferior parietal region is 15% larger than average, which could account for Einstein's superior visualization abilities. Making definitive (3) from these findings has been difficult, but the subject remains one of great interest and speculation. Members of the public can see slides containing small sections of Einstein's brain at the Mütter Museum in Philadelphia.

1. (   )   (A) having found   (B) find
            (C) to find   (D) finding

2. (   )   (A) who   (B) which
            (C) what   (D) how

3. (   )   (A) conclusions   (B) geniuses
            (C) physics   (D) institutions

Careers

5 Sports Medicine

Intense training and physical activity place great strains on athletes' bodies. Sports medicine professionals help people train, stay healthy, and recover from injuries. High-tech devices assist in the process, as does research into the causes of injuries and the best recovery methods.

Pre-Reading Questions Discuss these questions in pairs.

1. Do you play any sports? If so, have you ever worked with a specialist such as a trainer or nutritionist?

2. Some contact sports are risky, leading to head injuries and other serious problems. Can you think of anything that might help keep athletes safe?

3. More and more athletes are having their DNA tested to obtain a competitive advantage. How do you feel about that? Is it fair?

Vocabulary Warm-up   Track 14

A Read and listen to this list of the unit's target vocabulary. Write the letter of the target word or phrase next to the correct definition.

a. array	f. circulation	k. on the horizon
b. assess	g. convert	l. optimize
c. at stake	h. disseminate	m. regimen
d. bona fide	i. fatigue	n. rehabilitation
e. burgeoning	j. in conjunction with	o. surgeon

___ 1. doctor who performs operations

___ 2. send out; distribute

___ 3. coming in the near future

___ 4. together with

___ 5. range; variety

___ 6. tiredness

___ 7. analyze; consider

___ 8. growing; expanding

___ 9. genuine; real

___ 10. improve; make something as good as it can be

B Complete each sentence with the correct word or phrase from the list above. Remember to use the correct word form.

1. Olympians have demanding training _____ involving strict diets, workout routines, and practice sessions.

2. Before solar energy can be used in a home, the electricity must be _____ from DC to AC power.

3. If the home team wins, they will advance to the championship round, so there's a lot _____ with today's game.

4. The _____ program for her sprained ankle includes swimming laps.

5. When you're cold, rubbing your hands together improves _____.

Reading Passage Track 15

In professional and recreational sports, athletes are pushing themselves harder than ever. Sports medicine professionals serve important functions in keeping us healthy. They help prevent injuries, treat them when they occur, and assist athletes in **optimizing** their performance. Universities provide
5 vital contributions to the field through research, and companies produce high-quality equipment used in training **regimens**, competitive matches, and **rehabilitation** programs.

Sports medicine physicians are doctors with advanced training in areas like physiology and biomechanics. These highly educated specialists may work
10 for a professional team or at a hospital, with many serving as orthopedic **surgeons**. Other doctors specialize in treating children, who, because they are still growing, have a different physiology from adults. Besides common injuries like knee and shoulder sprains, kids sometimes suffer from overuse conditions like tendonitis.

15 Other professionals in the sports medicine field assist high schools, colleges, professional teams, and individuals. For example, athletic trainers set up rehabilitation programs for injured players; nutritionists help athletes maintain an optimal
20 weight; and physical therapists facilitate recovery from injuries. There's also a **burgeoning** demand for sports psychologists, who teach players to

In some contact sports, players are tackled many times per game.

manage stress, focus on goals, and stay motivated. As more elite athletes emerge as **bona fide** celebrities, with huge amounts of money **at stake** for teams
25 and players, it's no wonder there's a call for such extensive support networks.

Research is critical when it comes to keeping athletes healthy. In contact sports, concussions are common, which has led to far-ranging research into treatment and prevention efforts. For example, a group of bioengineers analyzed tackling patterns in rugby, finding that 77% of head injuries were
30 caused by impacting a player's upper trunk or upper legs. The group issued several recommendations, including tackling the lower trunk (near the pelvis area) to minimize the risk of injury.

Other studies of soccer and hockey players have looked at the usefulness of a device called the Q-Collar. Worn around the neck, it slightly presses on a
35 jugular vein, increasing the volume of blood in the brain and reducing the brain's movement during head impacts. The studies found the device to be

effective for both male and female athletes. When practical findings like these are **disseminated** to players, schools, coaches, and leagues, they can have widespread benefits.

40 There is already a large **array** of devices that optimize performance and reduce the risk of injury. For example, compression stockings worn by soccer players improve **circulation**, reduce **fatigue** (a leading cause of injuries), and boost endurance. During training, athletes can also wear sensors which track metrics like heart rate, temperature, and stress levels. Then there are movement trackers 45 which map a baseball pitcher's throwing motion and make recommendations to help prevent the elbow injuries that many players suffer from. There's even a growing selection of high-tech clothing with built-in sensors. The real-time data they generate is a boon to players and medical support staff.

Rehabilitation programs are also benefiting from technological advances. 50 Gaming software powered by virtual reality devices assists with recovery from neck injuries. AlterG's anti-gravity treadmill takes 20% to 100% of the weight off patients' bodies so they can build strength without putting pressure on injured areas. And, platelet-rich plasma therapy accelerates the recovery process by enriching an athlete's blood with nurturing properties. 55 Another cutting-edge therapy is laser biostimulation, which directs energy, in the form of photons, to the exact spot of an injury. The body absorbs the photons and **converts** them to healing chemical energy. The procedure does not require an incision, and there are no negative side effects.

These are a few of the many devices and procedures in use, and the future 60 is even more promising. Personalized genetic therapies may soon play a central role at every stage of an athlete's career, helping **assess** risks, prevent injuries, formulate precise nutritional plans, and more. Safety equipment **on the horizon** includes high-tech helmets that release bursts of air on impact, providing padding for your head like an airbag. As professional athletes 65 continue to smash records, and as more children and adults enjoy recreational sports, these advances, **in conjunction with** sports medicine professionals, will help us stay safe as we run, jump, dodge, and throw as quickly as we can.

---

9 biomechanics – the study of the body's movement and structure   10 orthopedic – related to the muscles, bones, etc.   14 tendonitis – the inflammation of a tendon   19 optimal – ideal
27 concussion – injury caused by a head impact   28 bioengineer – specialist who uses engineering knowledge to study the human body   29 tackle – grab or hit a player so that he or she falls
30 trunk – the upper part of one's body   35 jugular vein – a vein in the neck   48 boon – benefit
53 platelet – blood cell that helps stop bleeding   53 plasma – a part of the blood
55 biostimulation – growth supported by adding nutrients   56 photon – particle of light
62 formulate – create

Choose the best answer to each question.

.... Main Idea

1. (   ) What is the main idea of the reading?
   A. Preventing concussions is a top goal of sports medicine practitioners.
   B. Though more children are participating in sports, there is an insufficient number of physicians to treat them.
   C. Jogging, weightlifting, and playing team sports are heart-friendly activities.
   D. Doctors, medical specialists, universities, and private businesses contribute to the sports medicine field.

.... Detail

2. (   ) Which of the following reduces brain shaking when a player is tackled?
   A. AlterG's anti-gravity treadmill   B. Compression stockings
   C. Platelet-rich plasma therapy   D. The Q-collar

.... Vocabulary

3. (   ) In line 26, what does "contact" mean?
   A. physical impact   B. direct communication
   C. regular transmission   D. professional league

.... Analysis

4. (   ) What is a key reason why top athletes need the assistance of so many sports medicine professionals?
   A. There are significant financial considerations involved.
   B. Fans are insisting that elite players consult multiple specialists.
   C. League requirements have to be followed by every player.
   D. Nutritionists prefer to work alongside trainers and psychologists.

5. (   ) What does the article suggest about the future?
   A. Thanks to laser biostimulation, injured athletes will never need surgery.
   B. Helmets with airbag style properties will be completely invisible.
   C. Cutting-edge devices will be more vital than sports medicine physicians.
   D. Genetic therapies could soon be important in keeping athletes healthy.

Short Answers   Write a full-sentence answer to each question.

1. What are some sports-related medical problems that children have?

_____

2. How do sports psychologists help athletes?

_____

3. What are the benefits of using compression stockings?

_____

Vocabulary Building

A **Choose the answer that is a synonym for the word or phrase in italics.**

1. In the soccer world, Brazilian star Pelé is a *bona fide* legend.
   A. talented   B. genuine   C. nominated

2. *Fatigue* set in for most of the players towards the end of the long match.
   A. Excitement   B. Tiredness   C. Frustration

3. The stadium has an *array* of guest services, including a small clinic and a shower room.
   A. good range   B. costly decision   C. high rank

4. The committee issued its findings *in conjunction with* several international sports medicine organizations.
   A. regardless of   B. in advance of   C. together with

5. Athletes want to be strong, but they need to be careful not to overdo things with their workout *regimens*.
   A. objectives   B. teammates   C. routines

B **Complete each sentence below with one of these words or phrases. Remember to use the correct word form.**

> surgeon   on the horizon   disseminate   burgeoning   at stake

1. During the operation, the _____ will be assisted by three nurses.

2. Medical journals are an important means by which new findings and treatments are _____ to healthcare professionals.

3. The _____ interest in data-driven conditioning programs is boosting demand for wearable sensors.

4. A lot is _____ every time a star player takes the field, so teams make great efforts to keep them healthy and happy.

5. Thanks to advances in genetic research, personalized medication is _____. In the coming years, we will hear much more about it.

C **Choose the correct form of the words in parentheses.**

1. The VR program allows you to (optimize / optimization) your pitching motion.

2. Reporters gathered around the team physician to hear her (assess / assessment) of the star player's recovery progress.

3. The physical therapist who oversaw my (rehabilitation / rehabilitated) was very patient.

4. What's the (conversion / convert) rate from kilometers to miles?

5. When an artery is blocked, a person's blood does not (circulating / circulate) properly.

45

Focus on Language

Word Parts

Study the word parts in the chart below. Then read the pairs of sentences that follow. Decide if the second sentence is true or false.

Word Part	Meaning	Examples
ortho-	straight	orthopedics, orthodox
-mech-	machine; tool	mechanic, biomechanical
-itis	inflammation	bronchitis, arthritis

1. As a child, Brittany had several crooked teeth, so her parents took her to an orthodontist to get them fixed.

   The medical professional helped straighten her teeth. (True / False)

2. The doctor concluded that Hideo had tonsillitis, an easily treatable condition.

   According to the physician, Hideo's tonsils were smaller than normal. (True / False)

3. The bicycle company will cut costs by mechanizing most of the assembly process.

   In the future, the bicycles will largely be put together by machines. (True / False)

Grammar & Usage   *Adverb + Adjective/Past Participle + Noun*

This common structure provides a rich description of a noun. The noun is modified by an adjective or past participle, which is further modified by an adverb.

Ex: Massage is a particularly effective therapy for muscle pain.

Ex: It is a widely known fact that exercise contributes to good health.

Fill in the blanks with the correct form of the words in parentheses.

1. The chief surgeon is a _____ _____ (high, experience) physician.

2. I found the manual to be an _____ _____ (extreme, use) book with great tips and information.

3. The _____ _____ (expert, write) instructions make it easy for even novice mechanics to operate the diagnostic tool.

Listening Listen to the short talk. Then answer these questions.

Track 16

1. (   ) What is the purpose of this talk?
   - (A) To announce a medical breakthrough
   - (B) To give an injury update
   - (C) To provide a set of training instructions
   - (D) To advertise a clinic

2. (   ) Which of these facilities is NOT mentioned?
   - (A) A basketball court
   - (B) A 3D imaging system
   - (C) VR exercise equipment
   - (D) A swimming pool

3. (   ) When is Westlake closed?
   - (A) Tuesday at noon
   - (B) Wednesday at 3:00 PM
   - (C) Friday at 8:00 AM
   - (D) Saturday at 1:30 PM

Reading Fill in each blank with a word or phrase from each group below.

The International Federation of Sports Medicine, known by the acronym FIMS (derived from the original French name), was founded in 1928. It's a leading organization that is affiliated with the International Olympic Committee and the United Nations. (1), the FIMS has ties with sports medicine associations in 117 countries, representing 125,000 sports physicians.

The organization is active in promoting education in the field and encouraging scientific research, with important new findings (2) in the *International SportMed Journal*. The group also distributes the *FIMS Team Physician Manual*. In addition to meetings and conferences held at the regional level, the FIMS hosts a biannual World Congress, where doctors and other professionals (3) with colleagues.

1. (   )
   - (A) Furthermore
   - (B) Otherwise
   - (C) However
   - (D) Nevertheless

2. (   )
   - (A) publishing
   - (B) publishes
   - (C) to publish
   - (D) published

3. (   )
   - (A) substitute
   - (B) diagnose
   - (C) network
   - (D) reconsider

6 Culture

Cultural Awareness

In our native culture, we are accustomed to the way most people think and behave. It's more difficult to understand other cultures while avoiding stereotypes. However, the effort is worthwhile, since improving cultural awareness enriches our lives.

Pre-Reading Questions   Discuss these questions in pairs.

1. What is a good way to learn about other cultures?

2. What might be challenging about working in another country?

3. Over the last 10 years, have a lot of people from other countries moved to your area? If so, how has the change impacted daily life? (For example, have new stores or restaurants opened?)

Vocabulary Warm-up Track 17

A Read and listen to this list of the unit's target vocabulary. Write the letter of the target word or phrase next to the correct definition.

a. accurate	f. expand one's horizons	k. pitfall
b. acknowledge	g. interpret	l. prediction
c. affable	h. intersect	m. rapport
d. authority	i. nationality	n. unconscious
e. behavior	j. out of the ordinary	o. underpinning

___ 1. meet; cross

___ 2. broaden one's knowledge or interests

___ 3. relationship; bond

___ 4. correct

___ 5. automatic; instinctive; involuntary

___ 6. unusual; uncommon

___ 7. basis; foundation

___ 8. figure out; analyze

___ 9. friendly

___ 10. admit; recognize

B Complete each sentence with the correct word or phrase from the list above. Remember to use the correct word form.

1. Companies selling goods overseas often have trouble securing shelf space for their products. It's one of the _____ of international business.

2. In a library, making loud noises is unacceptable _____.

3. What's your _____ for the outcome of the soccer tournament?

4. As the managing director, only Mr. Garcia has the _____ to approve salary bonuses.

5. I believe Patricia's _____ is French, but she might be Swiss.

Reading Passage Track 18

In schools, offices, and stores, our shared spaces are becoming increasingly diverse and multicultural. People are also traveling, working, and studying abroad more than ever. This new reality exposes us to cultural differences on a regular basis. They encompass vibrant expressions of art, music, and
5   clothing, as well as the way we communicate, view **authority**, and much more. By improving our awareness of the way people from other countries see the world, we can bridge our differences and **expand our horizons**.

Everyone is born into a particular culture, which provides a framework for the way we act and **interpret** situations. These perspectives are manifested
10 in our speech, **behavior**, and gestures, which form important parts of our identity. It's common to become uncomfortable when encountering cultural expressions which are **out of the ordinary**. For example, let's say you are in another country on a train on which people are talking loudly. The situation might be unnerving. That's the point at which our upbringing **intersects** with
15 the realities of another culture, and we can either be upset or try to grasp the **underpinnings** of the situation.

One of the best starting points is an introspective look at your thoughts and feelings. It lets you identify the logic system of your own culture and
20 recognize any **unconscious** biases you may have. In the case of the train, you might **acknowledge** that the occurrence would be uncommon in your hometown. The next step is to observe how other passengers respond. If nobody seems to mind
25 the noise, it could be that your preconceptions of how train riders should behave are affecting your judgment.

Diverse workplaces may present challenges related to communication styles and cultural expectations.

Such a situation is a perfect opportunity to see things through another person's eyes – what anthropologists call the emic perspective. You can expand your
30 understanding further by listening and asking questions. Let's say you're working for a manager from another country, and you see an opportunity to improve a packaging design. In some cultures, making suggestions to a person in authority could be seen as disrespectful, whereas other cultures encourage such behavior. Asking a colleague for advice is one move you could make.
35 Though it may seem counterintuitive, admitting that we don't know something about another culture does not show weakness. On the contrary, "looking

before you leap" shows that you are open-minded and eager to learn about local practices.

When it comes to foreign colleagues and classmates, establishing comradery
40 can be tricky. Certain cultures value being modest and reserved, while others emphasize being open and **affable**, even with people you just met. Flexibility goes a long way with interpersonal dynamics. If you are uncomfortable opening up about yourself, just explaining that point provides a deeper understanding of your background while building **rapport**. It's worth
45 remembering that as hard as we work to understand other people's cultures, they may also struggle to understand ours.

One of the **pitfalls** in this process is stereotyping. The world is complex, and broad generalizations exist because they make it easier to filter and categorize information. However, even in countries with fairly homogenous populations,
50 there are significant differences between people and from region to region. Stereotypes, whether they are positive or negative, are rarely **accurate**.

In a large study involving people from six countries, German psychologists tested perceptions of other cultures' attitudes towards money. Everyone was given a small amount of money to share. Participants first made **predictions**,
55 ranking which **nationalities** they thought would be the least to the most generous. As it turned out, the pre-experiment rankings were the exact *opposite* of the amounts shared, proving the stereotypes completely wrong.

How, then, can we prepare for new cultural encounters? Reading books and websites is one method, but the tips they provide should be taken as general
60 ideas, not prescriptive rules. They can help you avoid mistakes, yet as the saying goes, experience is the greatest teacher. Maintain an open mind and realize that our differences make us stronger by adding diverse perspectives and contributions. Culture isn't a matter of right or wrong, and it isn't a competition. Loving where we are from while respecting other cultures, in
65 addition to maintaining a healthy curiosity, might be the keys to making us more informed global citizens.

---

9 manifest – make seen; reveal   14 unnerving – uncomfortable   14 upbringing – the way someone is raised   17 introspective – reflecting on your life and actions   20 bias – tendency to hold certain opinions or preferences   25 preconception – belief or opinion held before one has experienced something   29 anthropologist – person who studies humanity and its cultures
29 emic – cultural analysis from the perspective of a member of the culture being studied
35 counterintuitive – against expectations of what will happen   39 comradery – friendship; feeling of belonging   40 tricky – difficult; complex   42 dynamic – relationship structure
43 open up – reveal; share   49 homogenous – being the same   60 prescriptive – very strict or rigid

.... **Main Idea**

1. (   ) What is the main idea of the reading?
   A. People from Eastern and Western nations have a hard time understanding each other's cultures.
   B. Shops have signs in multiple languages to assist international visitors.
   C. Studying art and history are effective ways to improve cultural awareness.
   D. Learning about other cultures enriches our lives, but we should try to avoid mistakes in the process.

.... **Detail**

2. (   ) According to the article, which of these can help us make international friends?
   A. Flexibility   B. Stereotyping
   C. Aggression   D. Struggling

.... **Vocabulary**

3. (   ) In line 40, what does "reserved" mean?
   A. conservative   B. booked   C. occupied   D. kept

.... **Analysis**

4. (   ) Let's say you are overseas and people are pushing each other to board a bus. What might you learn by considering the emic perspective of other riders?
   A. The perspective of other visitors from your country
   B. The bus fares and schedules from a variety of countries
   C. The situation from the point of view of local bus riders
   D. The cultural importance of global transportation systems

5. (   ) How should a list of "cultural do's and don'ts" be treated?
   A. If written by someone who visited the country, it is probably correct.
   B. To avoid stereotypes, it's best to completely disregard the list.
   C. It could be useful, but it shouldn't be treated as a definitive list.
   D. In general, the more popular a list is, the more accurate it is.

Short Answers   Write a full-sentence answer to each question.

1. When it comes to cultural questions, what is the benefit of "looking before you leap"?

   _____

2. What did the German experiment prove about certain stereotypes?

   _____

3. How do our cultural differences make us stronger?

   _____

Vocabulary Building

A **Choose the answer that is a synonym for the word in italics.**

1. Your *nationality* goes on line 6 of the application.
   A. approval   B. itinerary   C. citizenship

2. When partnering with a company in another country, misunderstandings stemming from differing cultural assumptions are common *pitfalls*.
   A. downsides   B. languages   C. proposals

3. After her accident, Lisa developed an *unconscious* fear of motorcycles.
   A. temporary   B. involuntary   C. unrelated

4. Who has the *authority* to grant a contract extension?
   A. length   B. power   C. fame

5. The article's most interesting *prediction* concerns the economic importance of African nations in the late 21st century.
   A. correction   B. restriction   C. expectation

B **Complete each sentence below with one of these words or phrases. Remember to use the correct word form.**

out of the ordinary   rapport   intersect   underpinning   expand one's horizons

1. At the Museum of Urban Planning, art and design _____ with diverse architectural styles.

2. There's nothing _____ about the report, which is fairly typical.

3. Traveling to Ireland is a fantastic way to _____. You're going to have an amazing time.

4. The party is a chance for new employees to build _____ with their colleagues.

5. Trust is a central _____ of most friendships.

C **Choose the correct form of the words in parentheses.**

1. Can you please check the (accuracy / accurately) of these calculations?

2. Sometimes (acknowledgement / acknowledging) a mistake is the best way out of a difficult situation.

3. It takes a lot of skill to work as a simultaneous (interpretation / interpreter).

4. As the guests arrived, they were (affable / affably) greeted by their hosts.

5. (Behaviors / Behavioral) scientists seek out the reasons for the way we act.

Word Parts

Study the word parts in the chart below. Then read the pairs of sentences that follow. Decide if the second sentence is true or false.

Word Part	Meaning	Examples
up-	higher	upbeat, upwelling
-div-	separate	divide, indivisible
-fy	make; cause	rectify, simplify

1. According to these directions, the road will diverge in two kilometers.

   Up ahead, the number of lanes will decrease from two to one. (True / False)

2. The multilingual sign exemplifies the city's efforts to appeal to international visitors.

   It's an example of an attempt to attract people from other countries. (True / False)

3. Because of an upsurge in visa applications, processing times are longer – close to a month in some cases.

   The longer processing times are due to an increase in applications. (True / False)

Grammar & Usage   *Such & So*

Such emphasizes a noun, which may also be preceded by an adjective and/or an adverb. *So* emphasizes an adjective. *So* can also be used at the start of an adverb clause to explain something's reason.

Ex: It was <u>such</u> an uplifting speech. I'll send you a link to the video.

Ex: These brownies are <u>so</u> delicious!

Ex: We're sending out invitations early <u>so</u> they'll arrive in plenty of time.

Complete each sentence with *such* or *so*.

1. I was _____ surprised when I heard Rachel was getting married.

2. I never knew Mr. Lin was _____ a talented singer.

3. _____ that everyone can prepare for the meeting beforehand, I've put together a list of the topics we'll be covering.

Listening Listen to the short talk. Then answer these questions.

Track 19

1. (   ) How many different countries are the students from?
    (A) 7   (B) 11
    (C) 16   (D) 135

2. (   ) According to the speaker, what is Wilmore University's main goal?
    (A) To assist with students' language abilities
    (B) To help students excel in their schoolwork
    (C) To make sure everyone enjoys themselves
    (D) To expand the number of foreign students

3. (   ) Which of the following will NOT be at the party?
    (A) Music   (B) Food
    (C) Drinks   (D) Gift bags

Reading Fill in each blank with a word or phrase from each group below.

Cultural differences have real-world impacts on some of the most personal aspects of our lives, including healthcare. Hospitals with diverse patient bases are learning to respond to the ways people from other countries (1) medical decisions. For instance, some patients defer to the suggestions of their spouses or ask older relatives for advice. Religious considerations may also affect a patient's choice of treatments.

The American Academy of Family Physicians created a checklist to help doctors (2). For example, it asks whether doctors have information prepared in multiple languages. It also questions whether a doctor accepts that people from other backgrounds have different values (3) treatments. The checklist helps doctors improve their flexibility and recognize cultural biases.

1. (   )   (A) make   (B) making
            (C) having made   (D) to make

2. (   )   (A) expand their stereotypes (B) cure some diseases
            (C) immigrate to the country (D) address these issues

3. (   )   (A) above   (B) towards
            (C) through   (D) beside

7 Lifestyles

Living off the Grid

Cities are the cultural and financial centers of the modern world, partly because of their easy access to food, electricity, and important services. However, a shift is underway. More people are providing for their families in rural areas without giving up all the comforts of city life.

Pre-Reading Questions   Discuss these questions in pairs.

1. Why do you think some people are leaving cities and moving to rural areas?

2. How would you like to live in a place that's far from any urban areas?

3. If you had to grow your own food, what would you plant?

Vocabulary Warm-up Track 20

A Read and listen to this list of the unit's target vocabulary. Write the letter of the target word or phrase next to the correct definition.

a. amenity	f. forgo	k. self-sufficient
b. budget	g. install	l. susceptible
c. carbon footprint	h. orchard	m. utility
d. configuration	i. permit	n. viable
e. embrace	j. safety net	o. virtually

___ 1. group of trees that bear fruits or nuts

___ 2. luxury; special feature

___ 3. possible; suitable

___ 4. independent; able to take care of yourself

___ 5. do without

___ 6. amount of money available or planned

___ 7. welcome

___ 8. document saying you're allowed to do something

___ 9. nearly; almost

___ 10. set up; connect

B Complete each sentence with the correct word or phrase from the list above. Remember to use the correct word form.

1. Homes near the ocean are _____ to natural disasters like typhoons.

2. Riding a bicycle and recycling will reduce your _____.

3. We use a wind turbine to generate power, but we also have a diesel generator. It's a(n) _____ in case the turbine doesn't produce enough electricity.

4. The _____ company announced the price of natural gas will go up 2% next month.

5. A popular _____ for solar panels involves laying them on your roof. You can also place them in a sunny spot away from your home.

Over the last century, there has been a massive population shift to urban areas, which are convenient and exciting, yet crowded and expensive. With help from modern technology, more and more families are going the opposite direction, moving to the countryside to live peaceful, quiet lives. Those who
5   want to be completely **self-sufficient** go "off the grid," supplying their own power, water, food, and other daily needs.

Virtually every home in a town or city is connected by wires, pipes, and gas lines to public **utilities**. There are many reasons why people choose to **forgo** these **amenities** and make it on their own in a rural area. First, it's
10 environmentally friendly. By living in a small home and using renewable energy like solar power, you dramatically reduce your **carbon footprint**. The lifestyle is also healthier, since by growing your own food, you know exactly what's going into it. Plus, once the set-up costs have been paid, you'll save a lot on monthly expenses.

15 Transitioning to an off-grid lifestyle typically starts with buying a small plot of land, with two acres being adequate. You can move into a house that's already on the property, build a new home, or buy a pre-built "tiny home." For
20 example, Clayton manufactures the energy-efficient I-House, which has solar panels on the roof and excellent insulation. To install your own solar power system, you'll need solar panels, an inverter, and batteries to store power

Eating nutritious, garden-fresh produce is a major benefit of living off the grid.

25 for nighttime use. With a "grid-tied" system, you can stay connected to the grid and sell the utility company any excess electricity. That connection also provides a **safety net**, allowing you to draw power from the grid as needed.

Installing a wind turbine is another option for power generation. Alternatively, if your property has a stream or river running through it, you
30 could set up a micro-hydro system powered by flowing water. Yet another option is a geo-thermal heat pump, which uses underground heat to drive a steam turbine. The power solution that's right for you depends on your **budget**, usage habits, and local resources.

The next basic need is water. Digging a well, **installing** an electric pump, and
35 connecting a pipe to the home is a popular **configuration**. A hand crank can be added to the well for emergency purposes. A more affordable option is

collecting rainwater in a catchment tank. The downside is you are **susceptible** to water shortages during times of drought.

40 Next you'll need a food source, which has countless delicious possibilities. You might start with a small garden, growing basic crops like beans and tomatoes and later adding more seasonal vegetables for a continual food supply. Excess crops can be canned or preserved for future use. Adding a grape vine or **orchard** with fruit and nut trees is also **viable**. To expand your food selection, raising bees provides honey, and livestock are a source of eggs and dairy 45 products.

Finally, there's the matter of treating sewage, which is relatively simple. A septic tank connected to the toilet converts waste to clean water and then adds it to the soil. An even more affordable option is building an outhouse away from your home. The waste is composted, resulting in fertilizer that enriches 50 the soil. The drawback is you have to go out in the cold to use it.

Even with a good plan in place for moving off the grid, the process has its drawbacks. Some areas, especially those close to cities, require **permits** for everything from digging a well to building your home. You also have to get accustomed to a simple lifestyle while making do with less electricity. And 55 the upfront costs can be significant. However, to that point, technological advances are leading to lower prices for solar panels and other equipment.

In Europe, Asia, North America, and elsewhere, moving off the grid is a growing trend. Already, some 25 million people get their power from solar energy, and millions more benefit from wind power. There's plenty of room 60 for flexibility in deciding the best approach for one's family. Some people generate their own electricity while using water from the city. Others grow a small amount of food in container pots and buy the rest from farmers' markets. The lifestyle amounts to a mindset **embraced** by those who want to take charge of their lives and their family's well-being.

---

5 grid – network of power lines, water lines, etc.   11 dramatically – greatly   24 inverter – device that converts electricity from DC to AC power   28 turbine – device that generates electricity when spun around   30 hydro – related to water   31 geo-thermal – heat that comes from the Earth   35 crank – a tool that you operate by rotating it   37 catchment tank – container that collects and stores rainwater   38 drought – dry period during which there is little or no rainfall   44 livestock – animals like cows and chickens raised on a farm   46 sewage – waste from a toilet   47 septic tank – container that holds and processes toilet waste   48 outhouse – small structure containing only a toilet   54 make do – get by; survive   63 mindset – way of thinking

Choose the best answer to each question.

........Main Idea

1. (   ) What is the main idea of the reading?
   A. Families who live off the grid prefer to be far from other people.
   B. Cities provide us with water, electricity, and other important services.
   C. Technology improves our lives, whether we are on or off the grid.
   D. An off-grid lifestyle has benefits but takes work to set up and maintain.

........Detail

2. (   ) Which source of electricity for off-grid homes is NOT discussed?
   A. Gasoline   B. The sun
   C. Wind   D. Water

........Vocabulary

3. (   ) In line 16, what does "plot" mean?
   A. plan   B. area
   C. story   D. chart

........Analysis

4. (   ) What does the article imply about the costs of moving off the grid?
   A. Building a home is cheaper than buying a pre-built tiny home.
   B. Treating sewage is one of the biggest expenses a person will have.
   C. The cost of installing a solar power system is decreasing.
   D. Most families find it hard to afford all the required permits.

5. (   ) According to the article, what might you do after growing more strawberries than you can eat?
   A. Preserve the strawberries and eat them later
   B. Trade them to a neighbor for a different fruit
   C. Sell them online or at a nearby farmers' market
   D. Compost them and use the fertilizer for crops

Short Answers Write a full-sentence answer to each question.

1. In what way is moving off the grid healthier?

   _____

2. How do homes that rely on solar power get electricity at night?

   _____

3. What is the risk of using a catchment tank for your water supply?

   _____

Vocabulary Building

A Choose the answer that is a synonym for the word or phrase in italics.

1. Lawrence, who works as a plumber, maintains a special savings account as a *safety net* to draw from during slow work periods.
   A. investment plan   B. risky choice   C. backup option

2. Crops which are *susceptible* to cold weather may not survive harsh winters.
   A. preferable   B. vulnerable   C. remarkable

3. With this window *configuration*, we'll maximize the sunlight the house receives.
   A. pattern   B. energy   C. thickness

4. Being *self-sufficient* provides the advantage of having a continual electricity supply even when the power grid is down.
   A. self-reliant   B. self-important   C. self-aware

5. You'll need a *permit* from the county before laying down the pipes.
   A. perception   B. perspective   C. permission

B Complete each sentence below with one of these words or phrases. Remember to use the correct word form.

carbon footprint	utility	virtually	orchard	amenity

1. The _____ company said our water will be restored tonight.
2. Michiko has apple and orange trees in her _____.
3. _____ all of our neighbors will be at the New Year's Eve party.
4. Having a hot tub may be a(n) _____, but it's something we'd hate to live without.
5. One easy way for offices to reduce their _____ is by asking employees to use coffee mugs instead of paper cups.

C Choose the correct form of the words in parentheses.

1. (Install / Installing) the micro-hydro power system will take three days.
2. The contractor is assessing the (viable / viability) of using a wind turbine on the property.
3. Due to (budgetary / budgeter) constraints, we had to postpone the product launch.
4. I don't shop a lot, so after we move to the countryside, I won't mind (forgo / forgoing) trips to the mall.
5. At first, it might be hard for your children to (embrace / embraced) a rural lifestyle.

Focus on Language

Word Parts

Study the word parts in the chart below. Then read the pairs of sentences that follow. Decide if the second sentence is true or false.

Word Part	Meaning	Examples
down-	lower; beneath	downfall, downturn
-pop-	people	populous, unpopular
-cy	state; quality	urgency, decency

1. The area south of the bus station is lightly populated, so land there is affordable.

   A large number of people live in the area. (True / False)

2. Since we live near train tracks connecting a manufacturing region to the coast, freight trains pass by with great frequency.

   Trains hauling goods are often seen traveling through the area. (True / False)

3. Being in the middle of a four-month drought, we're downbeat about the size of the soybean yield.

   The next harvest will likely be better than expected. (True / False)

Grammar & Usage   *Else & Elsewhere*

Else refers to an additional noun – either a person, place, or thing. *Else* can also refer to an alternative choice. And it can mean "otherwise," as in "or else." *Elsewhere* refers to a different place.

Ex: We'd better ask someone <u>else</u> what the correct procedure is.

Ex: If the rain catchment system is ineffective, we'll try something <u>else</u>.

Ex: The property is far away, so we're considering land <u>elsewhere</u>.

Complete each sentence with *else* or *elsewhere*.

1. We need to start now, or _____ we won't finish before nightfall.

2. The chicken coop shouldn't be so close to the driveway. Let's set it up _____.

3. Besides batteries, what _____ do you need from the store?

Listening   Listen to the conversation. Then answer these questions.

Track 22

1. ( ) Why is the man considering selling his house?
   (A) He travels a lot.   (B) Boston is too cold.
   (C) His mom lives in Atlanta. (D) The home is in bad shape.

2. ( ) What is the woman concerned about?
   (A) The matter of parking a tiny home
   (B) The amount of work the man will miss
   (C) The drive from Boston to Atlanta
   (D) The space for all the man's belongings

3. ( ) What does the man say about Monarch's homes?
   (A) They have lots of room inside.   (B) They are mobile.
   (C) They come with solar panels.   (D) They are 6 x 6 meters.

Reading   Read this passage. Then answer the questions below.

Leaving cities to live off the grid is not a recent phenomenon. Since 1967, there has been a community of people living that way in Victoria, Australia. The 121-hectare area, located nine kilometers from the small city of Castlemaine, is called Chewton Bushlands. Thirty-five homes are situated on separate plots of land, with each family providing for its own needs. Some houses have indoor toilets, while others make do with outhouses. Some homes have new solar power systems, while others have older equipment that barely powers essential items. Neighbors help each other in times of need, and the community holds festive events such as a yearly Christmas party. Thanks to Chewton Bushlands' proximity to Castlemaine, children can attend school in the city.

1. ( ) How many houses are there in Chewton Bushlands?
   (A) 9   (B) 35
   (C) 67   (D) 121

2. ( ) What does the passage imply about the electricity supply?
   (A) All of the homes are connected to a mini solar power grid.
   (B) Each family chooses its own way to generate power.
   (C) A power line runs from Castlemaine to Chewton Bushlands.
   (D) Most of the equipment supplying the electricity is old.

3. ( ) Where are the children educated?
   (A) In Chewton Bushlands   (B) At home
   (C) In Castlemaine   (D) All over Victoria

The Performing Arts

8

The Actor's Craft

Acting requires masterful physical control, with every movement and word comprising part of a performance. Intense training is needed to learn the craft, and in-depth preparation goes into bringing a role to life. Numerous techniques have been developed to help actors refine their skills.

Pre-Reading Questions   Discuss these questions in pairs.

1. Who are your favorite actors?

2. What characteristics are needed to be a great actor?

3. What do you imagine an actor does to prepare for a role?

Vocabulary Warm-up Track 23

A Read and listen to this list of the unit's target vocabulary. Write the letter of the target word or phrase next to the correct definition.

a. audition	f. mannerism	k. refine
b. competitive	g. memorize	l. repertoire
c. craft	h. motivation	m. screenplay
d. enraging	i. nuanced	n. strike a balance
e. feather in one's cap	j. one-size-fits-all	o. strive

___ 1. making someone very angry

___ 2. purpose; reason for doing something

___ 3. book containing the lines spoken in a movie, TV show, etc.

___ 4. try very hard; aim for

___ 5. remember every word in a list, speech, etc.

___ 6. subtle; finely detailed and carefully done

___ 7. habit; custom

___ 8. tryout for an acting role, place in a band, etc.

___ 9. art; trade

___ 10. accomplishment; something to be proud of

B Complete each sentence with the correct word or phrase from the list above. Remember to use the correct word form.

1. The hat is _____. Adjust the band on the back to fit your head.

2. Even getting a position as an unpaid intern at a Hollywood studio is _____. Many aspiring actors are eager for the opportunity.

3. The horror film star took a role in a comedy to expand his _____.

4. When you work 60 hours a week, it's difficult to _____ between your professional and private lives.

5. The post-production editing process used to take six months. By _____ its methods, the studio reduced both the time and cost.

Reading Passage Track 24

We spend our entire lives becoming who we are. In the all-encompassing art form of acting, the performer **strives** to transform into a completely different person with a distinct story, purpose, and personality. To portray a character, an actor must assume a new identity, and once the work is done and another
5   role is found, the palette is cleansed and the cycle starts all over again. With many tools and techniques to help with the process, actors continuously **refine** their skills to perfect their **craft**.

Becoming a skilled actor requires a wealth of experience performing on stage or in front of a camera. The learning process often starts with high school
10   plays and musicals, college films, and local theatre groups, which are always eager for fresh talent. It's helpful to expand one's **repertoire** by trying out improvisation, comedy, drama, and other acting styles. Studying behind-the-scenes tasks like lighting, costuming, and stage design broadens an actor's knowledge base. Also, complementary skills like singing, dancing, and
15   playing an instrument are useful **feathers in one's cap**.

Most actors have formal training in the field. Besides the drama and acting degrees offered by universities, there are dedicated acting schools with courses taught by actors, writers, directors,
20   and other industry professionals. Many of these institutions, like the New York Film Academy, **strike a balance** between teaching theory and technical skills (such as projecting one's voice) with practical skills like preparing for an **audition**
25   and surviving in a **competitive** industry. At DePaul University's Theatre School, around 30 student productions are put on yearly. Students have plenty of opportunities to apply the tips, tricks, and methods they've learned.

Actors must have masterful control over their movements and facial expressions.

Speaking of methods, over the last century, numerous techniques have
30   been developed to help actors hone and execute their craft. One of the most prominent was created by the Russian maestro Konstantin Stanislavski. His method stresses the importance of understanding the internal life of a character – his or her background, impulses, and **motivations**. An actor learns to think and feel like the character to breathe life into the role.

35   Another popular technique was developed by the famed American acting coach Sanford Meisner. In it, an actor's raw emotions are of central

importance, and the aim is to make the performance truthful and believable. Instead of over-thinking things, actors should focus on interacting with their fellow performers.

40 "Method acting," pioneered by Lee Strasberg, is another widely used technique. To prepare for a scene, actors should draw from personal experiences. So, for instance, in a scene in which a character is very angry, the actor should channel an **enraging** memory from his or her life.

With so many schools of thought towards the craft, it's important to note 45 that there is no "**one-size-fits-all**" approach. A performer might incorporate elements of Stanislavski and Meisner, as well as tips from teachers, coaches, and directors, in whatever combination is the most effective.

Once an actor has landed a role, a great deal of preparation is required before the curtain rises or the camera rolls. Beyond the essential starting 50 point of **memorizing** one's lines, an actor must make the character a three-dimensional person with a particular back story, way of speaking, set of interests, and **mannerisms**. While these elements may not be included in the **screenplay**, they add **nuanced** layers to the performance – such as a way of brushing one's hair or stressing the pronunciation of certain words. 55 Researching the story's historical era is of great assistance. Learning about the trends, popular music, and fashions of the time provides valuable nuggets which flesh out the role.

Beyond these broad preparations, every scene has its own questions which must be answered. For instance, where was the character before 60 the scene began? What does he or she hope to achieve, and how will that be accomplished? In this complex sea of preparations, perhaps the most important task is to make the performance seem natural and effortless. That way, the audience can enjoy the show while being inspired, challenged, or perhaps even repulsed by the character. If an intellectual or emotional 65 connection has been made with the audience, it's an indication that the actor's hard work was well worth the effort.

[1] all-encompassing – comprehensive; including everything   [4] assume – take on
[5] the palette is cleansed – you start over with a fresh perspective   [14] complementary – going or fitting together well   [23] project – send out farther away   [30] hone – refine
[31] maestro – master   [36] raw – basic, natural, and unrefined   [48] land – get; obtain
[49] the curtain rises – the moment when a stage performance (like a play) begins
[50] three-dimensional – complete; whole   [51] back story – background; origin
[56] nugget – something small and valuable   [57] flesh out – make something more complete and well-rounded   [61] sea – group; world

Reading Comprehension — Choose the best answer to each question.

.... **Main Idea**

1. (   ) What is the main idea of the reading?
   - A. The craft of acting is more demanding than any other performing art.
   - B. Along with actors, directors are also very important to a movie's success.
   - C. Stanislavski has influenced many acting schools, coaches, and performers.
   - D. Actors bring roles to life thanks to extensive training and preparation.

.... **Detail**

2. (   ) What school of thought emphasizes using memories from your own life when performing?
   - A. The Meisner way of acting
   - B. The New York Film Academy
   - C. The Stanislavski technique
   - D. Strasberg's method acting

.... **Vocabulary**

3. (   ) In line 8, what does "wealth" mean?
   - A. deep interest
   - B. great amount
   - C. profitable work
   - D. unusual background

.... **Analysis**

4. (   ) What is NOT suggested as a way to become a better actor?
   - A. Learning a skill like playing an instrument
   - B. Taking on roles that one is unaccustomed to
   - C. Focusing exclusively on either film or theatre
   - D. Studying a technical area like stage lighting

5. (   ) What does the article imply about an actor's preparations for a role?
   - A. They mostly involve decisions about how to walk and move.
   - B. The script might not include detailed background information.
   - C. Since it takes time, limited effort should go towards preparations.
   - D. The director will supply most of the necessary instructions.

Short Answers — Write a full-sentence answer to each question.

1. What are three styles of acting that an actor might try?

   _____

2. When studying a role's historical period, what can an actor learn about?

   _____

3. When delivering a performance, what might be the most important task?

   _____

Vocabulary Building

A Choose the answer that is a synonym for the word or phrase in italics.

1. One of Juliette's unique *mannerisms* is the way she holds a fork while eating.
   A. motivations   B. references   C. habits

2. Glass blowing is an ancient *craft* which is still widely practiced.
   A. art   B. tool   C. tale

3. For an actor, winning an Academy Award is a significant *feather in his or her cap*.
   A. achievement   B. responsibility   C. engagement

4. Remember to bring your headshots to the *audition*.
   A. director   B. tryout   C. movie

5. The studio will send a copy of the *screenplay* to your agent.
   A. contract   B. script   C. schedule

B Complete each sentence below with one of these words or phrases. Remember to use the correct word form.

strike a balance	repertoire	nuanced	strive	one-size-fits-all

1. The acting academy does not use a(n) "_____" approach. Instead, each student works with an advisor to plan a schedule of courses.

2. Among the skills in the clown's _____, he is especially famous for juggling and unicycle riding.

3. Claudia practices daily since she is _____ to become an Olympian.

4. We want to _____ between making the scene exciting yet funny.

5. In the _____ performance, the actor really made you believe he was a 19th-century furniture maker.

C Choose the correct form of the words in parentheses.

1. (Memorizing / Memorization) such a long speech will take several days.

2. As the film was made with the support of the local historical society, we were highly (motivation / motivated) to preserve a sense of factual accuracy.

3. When the casting call went out for the famous director's new film, I knew there would be heavy (competitive / competition) for even the smallest roles.

4. The producer was (enraged / enraging) when coffee was spilled on the main set piece.

5. Thanks to recent software (refines / refinements), we can now make the computer-generated planet look realistic.

Focus on Language

Word Parts

Study the word parts in the chart below. Then read the pairs of sentences that follow. Decide if the second sentence is true or false.

Word Part	Meaning	Examples
im-	not	implausible, imperceptible
-vers-	turned	version, anniversary
-ette	smaller type; lesser	kitchenette, cassette

1. The new shop on Melrose Avenue specializes in celebrity statuettes.

   The figures are probably too large to fit inside most homes. (True / False)

2. Stan has an aversion to violent movie scenes.

   He likely turns away when there is violence in a film. (True / False)

3. The contract negotiation's main impasse is over the way the studio and actors will share revenues.

   There is agreement about the way both sides will divide profits. (True / False)

Grammar & Usage   *Whatever, Whenever, & However*

These common words have distinct usage differences. *Whatever* means "anything" or "no matter what." *Whenever* means "anytime" or "at such a time." *However* means "in any way" or "regardless of the way."

Ex: Please order <u>whatever</u> you like. Dinner is on me.

Ex: I'm happy to leave <u>whenever</u> the group is ready.

Ex: <u>However</u> we divide up the tasks, the job will take all day.

Complete each blank with *whatever, whenever,* or *however*.

1. The baseball game will resume _____ it stops raining.

2. _____ this shelf fits together, we will need a screwdriver.

3. _____ it costs, I really want that jacket.

Listening   Listen to the conversation. Then answer these questions.

Track 25

1. (   )   How do they describe the character?
   (A) Kind   (B) Cruel
   (C) Smart   (D) Lucky

2. (   )   What does the man say about acting?
   (A) It must affect actors' private lives.
   (B) It takes years of intense training.
   (C) It is just like every other career.
   (D) It helps to have a good director.

3. (   )   According to the woman, in general, why should we respect actors?
   (A) They can become rich and famous.
   (B) They all use method acting.
   (C) They are committed to their craft.
   (D) They devote time to charity.

Reading   Fill in each blank with a word or phrase from each group below.

The acting profession continues to grow and evolve. (1   ) traditional outlets like films, TV shows, and plays, an actor might appear in commercials, public service announcements, or corporate training videos. More recently, Web series (2   ) in prominence, as has voice acting. A role may have lines, or the performer might work as a non-speaking extra on a production.

In the US, actors earn on average $49,000 per year, while in the UK, the average take-home is roughly £36,000. Actors continually audition for new roles, and there are invariably more actors than available positions. It's a difficult, though rewarding career, if not monetarily then at least for the (3   ) of creating memorable performances.

1. (   )   (A) Thanks to   (B) With regards to
           (C) In addition to   (D) Belonging to

2. (   )   (A) to grow   (B) have grown
           (C) growing   (D) grown

3. (   )   (A) satisfaction   (B) exhaustion
           (C) patience   (D) awkwardness

Conservation

Eco-Packaging

As the Earth's population grows and more products are manufactured, the amount of waste that is generated continues to increase. Plastic items and packaging are a significant part of the problem. Fortunately, the technology exists to reduce plastic waste and the environmental harm it causes.

Pre-Reading Questions   Discuss these questions in pairs.

1. What kinds of things do you recycle every day?

2. What do you often throw away?

3. How can we reduce the amount of garbage created by people and businesses?

Vocabulary Warm-up Track 26

A Read and listen to this list of the unit's target vocabulary. Write the letter of the target word or phrase next to the correct definition.

a. account for	f. fertilizer	k. mutually exclusive
b. arable	g. garner attention	l. petroleum
c. attendee	h. in its infancy	m. statistic
d. commit to	i. insatiable	n. stop-gap
e. decompose	j. landfill	o. toxic

___ 1. number providing information and data

___ 2. very new; just started

___ 3. liquid used to make oil and other items

___ 4. break down into smaller and smaller parts

___ 5. place where garbage is buried

___ 6. suitable for farming

___ 7. unable to exist together

___ 8. promise to

___ 9. done as a short-term measure

___ 10. unable to be satisfied

B Complete each sentence with the correct word or phrase from the list above. Remember to use the correct word form.

1. The waste is _____, so it must be transported in sealed drums.

2. The supermarket _____ when it announced that its deli would switch to biodegradable packaging. Several reporters covered the announcement.

3. Packaging costs currently _____ 15% of our production budget.

4. When mixed in, the _____ adds nutrients to the soil, making it stronger and healthier.

5. At the end of the speech, the 600 _____ stood and clapped.

Reading Passage Track 27

The disposal of solid waste contributes to many environmental problems, including ocean pollution, global warming, and groundwater contamination. An estimated 65% of household waste consists of bottles, trays, and other food packaging. One promising way to reduce this problem is by switching to
5 biodegradable packaging. Unlike most types of plastic, which are **petroleum** based, "bio-plastics" use plants as feedstock, resulting in zero waste when packaging items are properly disposed of. At a time when disturbing environmental news dominates the headlines, this type of clean, green solution is a win-win-win for businesses, consumers, and the Earth.

10 At the root of the problem is our **insatiable** demand for plastic. Global annual use has jumped from five million tons in the 1950s to 230 million tons today. Packaging **accounts for** 37% of the total. Unfortunately, instead of being recycled, most of it is buried in **landfills** or washed out to oceans, resulting in grim **statistics**. The estimated 25 trillion pieces of ocean plastic waste are
15 responsible for an annual 100,000 marine animal deaths. Plastic bottles that are buried in landfills may take 1,000 years or longer to **decompose**. What's more, landfills create methane, a serious greenhouse gas, as well as leachate, a **toxic** liquid that pollutes the soil, groundwater, and nearby waterways.

Expanding recycling efforts is one positive step.
20 However, the recycling process requires energy, making it a **stop-gap** response rather than a long-term solution. A more promising answer is to replace PVC, polyethylene, and other oil-based plastics with eco-friendly bio-plastics. Lids,
25 bottles, and other bio-plastic items are made from natural materials found in plants like corn and sugar cane. Once used, the packaging can be discarded along with food waste. Next, everything

Besides polluting the oceans, plastic harms fish and marine animals which mistake it for food.

is composted and converted to **fertilizer**, which is then used to grow a new
30 batch of crops, making it a positive "closed loop" cycle.

One popular bio-plastic, PLA (polylactic acid), is made by companies like NatureWorks. NatureWorks converts plant starch into little pellets of PLA, resulting in a product which the company calls Ingeo. The pellets are used to make food containers, coffee capsules, produce bags, and many other items.
35 They have excellent properties required for food packaging, including a high level of flexibility, heat resistance, and flavor retention.

Businesses have already started putting these innovations to work. For
example, Taco Time is a quick service restaurant with 75 locations in the USA.
In response to a 2010 Seattle ordinance requiring such restaurants to have
40   bins for recycling and composting, Taco Time switched many items, including
plates, cups, and cutlery, to biodegradable materials. At the end of a meal,
customers simply place the contents of their trays into a bin marked "Compost
here." As a result of its efforts, the company's compost output increased
from 111 tons in 2010 to 1,855 tons in 2015. Meanwhile, sales increased 47%,
45   proving that environmentally friendly decisions and corporate profits are not
mutually exclusive.

International events with huge numbers of **attendees** are also going green.
In 2012 the London Olympics **committed to** making itself the first zero-waste
Olympics. NatureWorks provided 120 million pieces of paper and plastic
50   packaging, including 14.3 million cups and 7.5 million hot drink lids. Again
the effort was a resounding success. The discarded waste was composted in
less than nine weeks, resulting in a large amount of fertilizer for local crops.

Despite these benefits, bio-plastics face criticisms and hurdles. As their use
expands, more **arable** land is devoted to growing feedstock. Widespread
55   land clearance has ecological implications for local wildlife. Furthermore,
items made from materials like PLA must be sent to industrial plants to be
composted. There's also the matter of educating the public. Though people
are accustomed to recycling glass and PET bottles, bio-plastics are not yet
widely familiar. Therefore, clear labels need to be placed on packages, and
60   municipal waste disposal systems need to be updated to handle collection and
composting.

The field of eco-packaging is **in its infancy**, but it has tremendous potential.
Other bio-plastics such as PHA are **garnering attention**. Also, items like
shipping supplies are being made from bio-plastics. Companies are even
65   developing edible packaging for food items. As we race to stop global
warming and clean up the environment, these creative solutions may go a
long way towards helping us save the planet.

---

[5] biodegradable – able to break down with the aid of microorganisms   [6] feedstock – raw material
used to produce something   [14] grim – sad; terrible   [17] greenhouse gas – gas such as CO_2 that
worsens global warming   [22] promising – hopeful   [29] compost – break down organic material
and convert it to fertilizer   [30] closed loop – starting and ending in the same place
[32] starch – energy source in the form of glucose   [32] pellet – small ball   [36] retention – holding;
keeping in   [39] ordinance – law   [51] resounding – loud and clear   [55] ecological – related to
living creatures and their habitats   [55] implication – consequence   [60] municipal – related to a
city or town

Choose the best answer to each question.

.... **Main Idea**

1. (　) What is the main idea of the reading?
   A. PHA may be a better bio-plastic than PLA.
   B. Eco-packaging could help solve major environmental problems.
   C. We should all try hard to reduce, reuse, and recycle what we use.
   D. The London Olympics was a zero-waste event.

.... **Detail**

2. (　) Every year, how many animals in the ocean die because of plastic waste?
   A. 1,000   B. 100,000
   C. 37 million   D. 25 trillion

.... **Vocabulary**

3. (　) In line 35, what does "properties" mean?
   A. characteristics   B. goods
   C. buildings   D. formalities

.... **Analysis**

4. (　) What can we infer about polyethylene?
   A. It does not result in the production of leachate.
   B. It is a commonly used bio-plastic.
   C. It is worse for the environment than PET.
   D. It may take 1,000 years to decompose.

5. (　) What followed Taco Time's switch to biodegradable packaging?
   A. A flattening of profits
   B. A rise in customer complaints
   C. An increase in sales
   D. A decline in compost output

Short Answers **Write a full-sentence answer to each question.**

1. In terms of reducing plastic waste, why is recycling a stop-gap response?

   _____

2. What are NatureWorks' Ingeo pellets used for?

   _____

3. How are items which are made of PLA composted?

   _____

Vocabulary Building

A **Choose the answer that is a synonym for the word or phrase in italics.**

1. Landfills *account for* 6% of the methane released into the atmosphere.
   A. reduce by   B. argue against   C. are responsible for

2. Many of the dinner *attendees* are environmental activists.
   A. guests   B. protesters   C. waiters

3. Since the chemical is highly *toxic*, it cannot be used in consumer products.
   A. poisonous   B. restricted   C. monitored

4. PHA is *garnering attention* because it is a naturally occurring bio-plastic.
   A. becoming cheaper   B. avoiding criticism   C. attracting interest

5. The practice of restaurants using bio-plastics for cutlery is *in its infancy*.
   A. just starting   B. generally misunderstood   C. becoming popular

B **Complete each sentence below with one of these words or phrases. Remember to use the correct word form.**

> petroleum   stop-gap   fertilizer   arable   mutually exclusive

1. Gardeners create _____ by composting food waste in backyard pits.

2. Because highways disrupt wildlife, building roads and protecting ecosystems are generally _____.

3. When drilling for _____ increases, the price of oil tends to fall.

4. Placing screens in rivers to stop plastics from flowing into oceans is a(n) _____ solution. We need to prevent the initial waste from occurring.

5. Thanks to its ideal climate, California has an abundance of _____ land.

C **Choose the correct form of the words in parentheses.**

1. Microorganisms aid in the (decompose / decomposition) of bio-plastics.

2. (Statistic / Statistically), buying vegetables from local farms creates a smaller carbon footprint than buying them from distant places.

3. After surviving for three days in the desert without water, the travelers drank (insatiably / insatiable) upon finding a water source.

4. While most corporations say they are (commit / committed) to environmental protection, consumers remain skeptical about "all-natural" product labels.

5. Two of the world's largest (landfill / landfills) are near Seoul and Los Angeles.

Focus on Language

Word Parts

Study the word parts in the chart below. Then read the pairs of sentences that follow. Decide if the second sentence is true or false.

Word Part	Meaning	Examples
poly-	many	polymer, polyglot
-grad-	step; degree	graduate, centigrade
-way	route; path	walkway, highway

1. The software has a retrograde feature letting you open files made in previous versions.

   To work on older files, you have to purchase additional software. (True / False)

2. In terms of marriage, it's one of the few countries where polygamy is still practiced.

   The country allows people to have more than one husband or wife. (True / False)

3. The passageway goes beneath the station's entrance and emerges on the other side.

   It's a path from one side of the station to the other. (True / False)

Grammar & Usage   *Passive Voice + Infinitive*

This structure shows how two actions are related. The first action leads to the second. The structure often involves verbs like "do, create, design," and "use."

Ex: The sign's red letters <u>are designed to attract</u> your attention.

Ex: The recycling bin <u>was moved to improve</u> its visibility.

Using the two verbs in parentheses, fill in the blanks with the *passive voice + infinitive*. The verb tense which should be used is also given.

1. Our new campaign _____ _____ _____ _____
   (design (present tense)...educate) people about the benefits of clean oceans.

2. Last year's revisions to the waste collection procedures _____
   _____ _____ _____ (make (past tense)...encourage)
   restaurants to compost their garbage.

3. _____ these screens _____ _____ _____ (install (past
   tense)...prevent) garbage from flowing into the ocean?

Listening Listen to the short talk. Then answer these questions.

Track 28

1. (   ) Where is the SGF handing out fact sheets?
      (A) In South Korean high schools
      (B) In 120 countries
      (C) On university campuses
      (D) At their group headquarters

2. (   ) What is global annual landfill waste expected to be in 2100?
      (A) 18,000 tons   (B) 20 million tons
      (C) 1.3 billion tons   (D) 4 billion tons

3. (   ) What does the SGF want young people to do?
      (A) Help clean up the Sudokwon Landfill
      (B) Produce stories about the environment
      (C) Talk to older people about global issues
      (D) Reduce the amount of waste they create

Reading Fill in each blank with a word from each group below.

Like regular plastics, bio-plastics are made through the process of polymerization. It involves linking together long strands of identical molecules. For example, to make the polymer (1   ) as PLA (polylactic acid), lactic acid molecules are joined into lactide rings. These rings are then linked together, forming a strong and durable material.

After a bio-plastic item – such as a PLA lid – is used, the process by which it decomposes involves two stages. First, the carbon bonds holding the long polymer chain together are broken down into smaller strands. Next, these strands are (2   ) by microorganisms as an energy source. The resulting material is a nutrient-rich fertilizer (3   ) can be added to soil to make it stronger, healthier, and more disease resistant.

1. (   )   (A) known   (B) called
            (C) named   (D) said

2. (   )   (A) explained   (B) afforded
            (C) imagined   (D) consumed

3. (   )   (A) who   (B) what
            (C) that   (D) where

10 Business Trends

Pop-up Shops

Thanks to the Internet and changing consumer preferences, the way we shop is undergoing a significant transformation. Pop-up shops, which are becoming common, stay open just a few weeks or months. The most successful ones creatively design and market their stores.

Pre-Reading Questions

Discuss these questions in pairs.

1. When you go shopping, what is the most important thing to you? Is it the price of items? The design of the store? Something else?

2. How can small stores attract more customers?

3. Have you ever been to a temporary shop? If so, what was it?

Vocabulary Warm-up Track 29

A Read and listen to this list of the unit's target vocabulary. Write the letter of the target word or phrase next to the correct definition.

a. amusing	f. entice	k. kiosk
b. blame	g. exclusive	l. marketing
c. brick-and-mortar store	h. go bankrupt	m. surge
d. consequence	i. journalist	n. sustainable
e. demographic	j. keep pace	o. volatile

___ 1. only available at a certain store, website, etc.

___ 2. advertising and selling

___ 3. maintain the same speed or level as others

___ 4. reporter

___ 5. sharp rise or growth

___ 6. physical shop

___ 7. attract

___ 8. small booth at a mall, festival, etc.

___ 9. funny

___ 10. result

B Complete each sentence with the correct word or phrase from the list above. Remember to use the correct word form.

1. Below-average sales were _____ on the poor weather.

2. Raw material prices can be _____, rising or falling 30% in a short period due to changing economic conditions.

3. Because of its huge debt load and falling revenues, the steel maker was forced to _____.

4. Companies that continually spend more than they earn do not have a(n) _____ business model.

5. Our main _____ is women aged 21-27.

Reading Passage Track 30

One of the **consequences** of the Digital Age has been a disruption of the traditional retail sales model. **Brick-and-mortar stores** are facing stiff competition from e-tailers like Amazon, and profits are being squeezed by savvy customers shopping for the lowest prices. One response has been
5 a **surge** in temporary retail outlets, commonly called pop-up shops. They provide low-risk opportunities for new and established brands while offering customers exciting shopping experiences.

The market has been so **volatile** in the early 21st century that thousands of big-box stores have shut their doors, with many chains **going bankrupt**. This
10 "retail apocalypse" saw 6,400 large shops close in the US just in 2017. Shifting consumer habits are partly to **blame**. For example, not only have bookstores and music shops struggled to **keep pace** with the large selections and low prices offered by e-tailers, but they have been impacted by the rise in digital media. Meanwhile, traditional department stores, once the anchor properties
15 driving traffic to malls, have enormous fixed costs that are no longer **sustainable**.

Although more than 90% of sales still occur at physical locations, many people, especially the younger **demographic**, are looking for personal
20 and interesting shopping experiences. Pop-up shops, which generally stay open from a few days to a few months, perfectly meet this need. They take a variety of forms, including store fronts, **kiosks**, food trucks, gallery spaces, booths at
25 festivals, and spaces within existing stores, known as "pop-in" shops. Specialty websites make it easy for brands to find locations to lease. Shop owners can even rent furniture, shelves, and fitting rooms to keep costs down.

Food trucks and kiosks, which are very popular, may be set up at events or parked on the street.

Saving money is one of the main advantages of running a pop-up shop. It
30 has been estimated that opening a temporary location costs 80% less than a permanent one. Artists, as well as online brands and small manufacturers, love this model since it lets them affordably grow their market and meet customers face-to-face. For example, in London the Poundshop provides exposure for artists and designers, who sell items for just 1 to 10 pounds.
35 Well-established brands also use pop-ups to test new products and generate buzz. Underwear maker Fruit of the Loom launched an **amusing** foray into

the high-end market with a pop-up called Früt. Garments were not only expensive, but they were hung from ostentatious tree displays to create a sense of luxury.

40 One of the secrets of pop-ups is using out-of-the-box thinking to **entice** and delight shoppers. Snarkitecture, a design studio, created a one-of-a-kind shop for clothing maker COS Los Angeles. The store was divided into two identical halves: one white and one pink, creating a mood that made a deep impression on shoppers. In several UK cities, frozen food maker Birds Eye opened
45 temporary restaurants called the Picture House to spread the word about its Inspirations meal line. When it came time to pay, no money exchanged hands. Diners simply took photos of their meals and posted them on Instagram with the hashtag #BirdsEyeInspirations. It was a case study in brilliant **marketing**.

Speaking of marketing, that is paramount when getting the word out about a
50 pop-up shop. Brands use websites and social media to reach their established bases. Hiring influencers on sites like YouTube and Instagram to promote the shop expands the reach, as does targeted advertising through Facebook and print media. One can also invite local **journalists** to preview the shop, leading to free marketing. Pop-ups frequently host launch parties for members of the
55 press and fans, with everyone encouraged to post photos and videos on social media. Shops continue generating traffic after opening by hosting workshops and exhibitions. For instance, Hutch LA's pop-up shop featured live T-shirt printing, with **exclusive** designs made on the spot.

Globally, the size of the temporary retail industry has been estimated at $22
60 billion, spread throughout Asia, Europe, and North America. As pop-up shops become mainstream, it's clear that to survive in today's unpredictable retail environment, brands need to be more flexible than ever. The most successful may be those with multichannel strategies, which could include a website, social media presence, and physical retail space. Staying relevant and
65 successful means being willing to change with the times while maintaining a commitment to quality and customer service.

---

3 squeeze – reduce; pressure   4 savvy – clever   9 big-box – large retail
10 apocalypse – period of extreme suffering and destruction   14 anchor property – main store attracting customers   35 generate buzz – bring attention to what you are doing
36 foray – campaign; exploration   37 garment – clothing item   38 ostentatious – extremely bold and flashy   40 out-of-the-box – creative; not standard   49 paramount – of top importance
49 get the word out – let people know about   51 influencer – person (often on social media) followed by many fans   53 print media – printed publications such as newspapers and magazines
58 on the spot – immediately done at a location

Reading Comprehension   Choose the best answer to each question.

.... **Main Idea**

1. (   ) What is the main idea of the reading?
    A. In the Digital Age, e-tailers are as influential as physical shops.
    B. Booths and other pop-up shops perform best at music festivals.
    C. Pop-up shops are a popular retail option for brands of all sizes.
    D. Due to their small inventories, pop-up shops must be temporary.

.... **Detail**

2. (   ) Which of these brands gave away meals to promote a product line?
    A. Hutch LA   B. Fruit of the Loom
    C. COS Los Angeles   D. Birds Eye

.... **Vocabulary**

3. (   ) In line 2, what does "stiff" mean?
    A. strong   B. recent
    C. inflexible   D. profitable

.... **Analysis**

4. (   ) Which of these would be considered a "pop-in" shop?
    A. A kiosk selling shirts and hats in a mall
    B. A booth with scented candles for sale inside a shoe store
    C. A food truck parked outside a stadium
    D. A website with a limited-time sale on living room goods

5. (   ) What does the article imply about pop-up shops' policies on customers taking photos?
    A. Taking photos is only allowed during opening parties.
    B. Photography is usually prohibited at events like workshops.
    C. Shops are happy for customers to take and share photos.
    D. All stores encourage the use of hashtags when posting photos.

Short Answers   Write a full-sentence answer to each question.

1. For pop-up shop owners, what is the advantage of renting items like furniture?

2. How do brands spread the message about pop-ups to their established bases?

3. What might be included in a brand's multichannel strategy?

Vocabulary Building

A **Choose the answer that is a synonym for the word in italics.**

1. Products which appeal to a wide *demographic* have the potential to be very successful.
   A. economic indicator   B. management team   C. population sector

2. As long as our factories continue operating efficiently, we believe the current production schedule is *sustainable*.
   A. affordable   B. debatable   C. maintainable

3. Some of the most successful commercials are *amusing* and creative.
   A. funny   B. thoughtful   C. dynamic

4. The most popular *kiosk* at the Earth Day event sold fresh fruit juice.
   A. drink   B. stall   C. guest

5. After the phone maker improved battery life by 75%, it saw a *surge* in sales.
   A. quick growth   B. prompt report   C. expected response

B **Complete each sentence below with one of these words or phrases. Remember to use the correct word form.**

| brick-and-mortar store | keep pace | marketing | go bankrupt | blame |

1. To _____ with our rivals, we should increase the number of cookies per box.

2. The manager was not looking for someone to _____ for the fall in productivity. Instead, she wanted the whole team to turn things around.

3. Some customers prefer "webrooming," which involves looking at items online and then buying them at a _____.

4. Once a company _____, its assets may be sold to pay back creditors.

5. Half of our _____ budget is designated for online ads.

C **Choose the correct form of the words in parentheses.**

1. As more firms enter the sector, some price (volatile / volatility) is to be expected.

2. The shoes are available (exclusively / exclusivity) at the pop-up shop.

3. Because pedestrians are (enticed / enticingly) by flashing signs, many stores use them.

4. (Journalistic / Journalism) has the power to change the world through in-depth investigative reporting.

5. The ceiling started leaking last week. (Consequently / Consequences), we had to close the salon until a plumber could repair the damage.

Focus on Language

Word Parts

Study the word parts in the chart below. Then read the pairs of sentences that follow. Decide if the second sentence is true or false.

Word Part	Meaning	Examples
apo-	away from	apology, apostrophe
-temp-	time	tempestuous, extemporize
-ice	with a certain quality	novice, precipice

1. Paul acquired his sense of justice from his father, who was in law enforcement.

   Paul's dad taught him about fairness. (True / False)

2. Niccolò Paganini, a contemporary of Beethoven, was a composer and virtuoso performer.

   The two composers lived at the same time. (True / False)

3. The IBEX satellite is 320,000 kilometers from the Earth at its apogee.

   At one point, the satellite is twice that distance from our planet. (True / False)

Grammar & Usage   *The various uses of "once"*

Once can appear at the start of a phrase describing the way something used to be. It can mean "when" in an adverb clause. And it can indicate frequency. Used on its own, it means "one time."

Ex: Mr. Reynolds was <u>once</u> a professional athlete.

Ex: Please let me know <u>once</u> the pallet arrives.

Ex: We drive up to the lake <u>once</u> a month.

Put the words in the correct sentence order.

1. (busiest / once the / in the country / airport / This was).

   _____

2. (is / the analysis / We will share / complete / our conclusion once).

   _____

3. (to the / a week / Mail / remote island once / is delivered).

   _____

Listening Listen to the short talk. Then answer these questions.

Track 31

1. (   ) Who is Jenny T?
   - (A) A reporter
   - (B) An influencer
   - (C) A hat collector
   - (D) A designer

2. (   ) What does the speaker say about the hats being made on site?
   - (A) All of the hats look the same.
   - (B) Customers can choose the color.
   - (C) There is a low launch party price.
   - (D) Someone takes a photo of your hat.

3. (   ) What piece of information is NOT given about the shop?
   - (A) Its website
   - (B) Its location
   - (C) Its hours of operation
   - (D) Its opening duration

Reading Read this article. Then answer the questions below.

With so many online brands creating niche products, competition for customers is fierce. That's why hiring social media influencers has become a popular marketing technique. Websites like Klout and Followerwork connect brands with local influencers, some of whom are very popular. Social media leaders on sites like Instagram and YouTube may have hundreds of thousands or even millions of followers. Just by wearing a jacket or recommending a product, they can give manufacturers a significant sales boost. In preparation for a pop-up shop's opening, a brand might hire an influencer to post a photo featuring one of its products. The celebrity might also provide details about the shop to his or her fans and may even make an appearance at a launch party.

1. (   ) Why would a brand use Klout?
   - (A) To locate a place to rent
   - (B) To rebuild a website
   - (C) To find an influencer to hire
   - (D) To collect market data

2. (   ) What does the passage state about social media influencers?
   - (A) Their fan bases may include millions of people.
   - (B) They often work for free if they like a brand.
   - (C) Many of them have their own clothing lines.
   - (D) There are more on YouTube than Instagram.

3. (   ) Which of these services provided by influencers is NOT discussed?
   - (A) Showing a product on social media
   - (B) Attending an opening party
   - (C) Providing information about a store
   - (D) Creating an exclusive design

11 Growing Up

Screen Time

At home, work, and many other places, we use digital devices from morning until night. The hours of "screen time" for adults keeps growing. Research shows that for children, we need to be especially careful about their use of phones and other devices.

Pre-Reading Questions   Discuss these questions in pairs.

1. Devices with screens, such as cell phones and computers, are everywhere. How do you feel about that?

2. Have you ever seen a very young child using a cell phone or tablet computer?

3. For children, what is one positive and one negative point about digital media like cartoons, video games, and mobile apps?

Vocabulary Warm-up Track 32

A Read and listen to this list of the unit's target vocabulary. Write the letter of the target word or phrase next to the correct definition.

a. anxiety	f. diligent	k. outlet
b. assertion	g. enable	l. threshold
c. at one's fingertips	h. exception	m. tolerance
d. cognitive	i. interfere	n. ubiquitous
e. crucial	j. mitigate	o. vie for

___ 1. seen everywhere

___ 2. very important; necessary

___ 3. close by; accessible

___ 4. certain level or point

___ 5. claim; declaration

___ 6. make something less problematic or serious

___ 7. compete for

___ 8. related to mental functions

___ 9. make possible; allow

___ 10. respect for and acceptance of diverse ideas, people, etc.

B Complete each sentence with the correct word or phrase from the list above. Remember to use the correct word form.

1. Since flooding is a problem in this neighborhood, we need to be _____ about keeping the storm drains clear of debris.

2. The noise from the busy street is _____ with my sleep patterns.

3. Animals aren't allowed into the restaurant, with the _____ of service animals like guide dogs.

4. Emilia suffered from _____ due to her stressful work environment.

5. Drawing is a creative _____ for countless children.

Digital screens are a **ubiquitous** feature of the modern landscape, with phones, computers, TVs, and other devices **vying for** our attention. With virtually unlimited information sources, time-saving tools, and entertainment options **at our fingertips**, there are clear advantages to this seismic lifestyle
5   shift. However, there are also reasons for concern, particularly when it comes to children. As we speed along in the Digital Age, we need to be **diligent** about moderating the content children consume and the amount of time they spend looking at screens.

For kids of all ages, digital media has positive aspects. High-quality TV shows
10 and movies promote pro-social skills like learning empathy and **tolerance**. Apps and websites **enable** learning about new subjects, involvement in civic activities, and participation in volunteer groups. Social media helps teenagers make and maintain friendships, form identities, and project a positive self-image. Devices are also imaginative **outlets** for creating music, videos,
15 artwork, and stories. Even video games have a positive side. Interacting with peers, lowering stress, achieving goals, and learning cooperative skills are among their strong points.

Despite these benefits, excessive screen time is discouraged. The American Academy of Pediatrics
20 (AAP) recommends that children under two years old avoid screens altogether, with the **exception** of video chatting with relatives. One reason is babies don't understand what they see on TV shows. Also, research by neuroscientists has shown
25 that small children learn more effectively by interacting with people than by watching videos. Finally, there is a downside to using devices to

By watching TV with their children, parents can point out and discuss what they see.

distract or pacify infants when they are upset. Babies are better off learning to deal with negative emotions and calm down on their own.

30 For kids 2-5 years old, the AAP recommends a daily maximum of one hour of high-quality programs like *Sesame Street*. Parents should co-watch shows with kids, discussing what they see to help them process the content. Going beyond the hour **threshold** takes time away from physical activity, spending time with friends, and reading with parents, all of which are **crucial**. Research
35 backs these **assertions** up. A Canadian study of 2-3 year olds found that kids with excessive exposure to digital media went on to score worse on

developmental tests when they were 3-5 years old. Problem solving, motor skills, and social skills all suffered.

As kids enter the pre-teen stage, parents need to remain vigilant, with 1-2
40 hours of entertainment screen time seen as a healthy amount. Staying below the limit reduces the risk of obesity, allows enough time for sleep, and helps maintain focus on schoolwork. What's more, a US study of 4,500 children aged 8-11 found that kids with more than two hours a day of screen time scored lower on **cognitive** tests. Memory, mental processing speed, and the ability to
45 pay attention were all impaired.

For teenagers, the digital landscape is more complicated, especially since the majority of teens have their own cell phones. Social media presents risks like cyber bullying, **anxiety**, and depression, not to mention privacy issues resulting from over-sharing. Parents are encouraged to help choose content
50 and discuss any problems teens encounter. Video games also need attention, since violent games can lead to aggressive, anti-social behavior. Excessive gaming runs the risk of addiction, which is so widespread that there's a term for it: Internet gaming disorder.

In the face of these challenges, researchers have created guidelines to help
55 families make sense of it all. It starts with a media plan for children and parents to follow. That includes setting up media-free areas, with experts putting kids' bedrooms at the top of the list, especially towards bedtime. Phones and other devices should be put away during meals and play times. Since TVs are distractions which **interfere** with family communication, they
60 should be turned off when not in use.

When it comes to digital media, the genie may be out of the bottle, but that doesn't mean we are powerless. Starting when children are very young, parents can make responsible choices and provide guidance. As children age, and even when they become teenagers who are inseparably attached
65 to their phones, the dialogue about screen time should continue. That way, the tremendous benefits of digital media can be enjoyed, and the potentially harmful aspects can be **mitigated**.

---

[4] seismic – very large   [7] moderate – manage   [7] consume – take in; digest
[11] civic – related to one's community   [19] pediatric – related to children (especially their medical issues)   [24] neuroscientist – specialist who researches the brain
[28] pacify – calm down; soothe   [35] back...up – support   [37] motor skill – ability related to movement   [39] vigilant – attentive; watchful   [41] obesity – the state of being very overweight
[45] impair – harm; negatively affect   [54] in the face of – considering; dealing with
[61] the genie is out of the bottle – something is here, and we can't make it go away
[64] inseparably – unable to be apart

Reading Comprehension   Choose the best answer to each question.

.... **Main Idea**

1. (   ) What is the main idea of the reading?
   A. Using digital media has both positive and negative sides for children.
   B. Because of the risks, children should avoid devices like cell phones.
   C. Everyone should participate in civic activities and volunteer efforts.
   D. Research about screen time has raised questions about video games.

.... **Detail**

2. (   ) For which age range is a total of one hour of daily screen time recommended?
   A. 0-2 years old   B. 2-5 years old
   C. 8-11 years old   D. 13-18 years old

.... **Vocabulary**

3. (   ) In line 32, what does "process" mean?
   A. administer   B. choose
   C. understand   D. replace

.... **Analysis**

4. (   ) What does the article imply about *Sesame Street*?
   A. It's best if parents and children watch it together.
   B. It is the highest-quality program on TV.
   C. Only certain episodes promote pro-social skills.
   D. Kids love toys based on the characters.

5. (   ) Which of these statements would most likely be part of the recommended screen time guidelines for families?
   A. Parents can use their phones during family discussions, but kids can't.
   B. Only pro-social TV shows should be watched before sleeping.
   C. At dinnertime, phones and tablets should not be on the dining table.
   D. The TV can be left on all the time as long as the volume is low.

Short Answers   Write a full-sentence answer to each question.

1. For teenagers, what are the benefits of social media?

   _____

2. What are the AAP's screen time guidelines for children under two years old?

   _____

3. What cognitive abilities were found to be impaired for 8 to 11-year-old children with more than two hours a day of screen time?

   _____

Vocabulary Building

A **Choose the answer that is a synonym for the word in italics.**

1. Did the speaker have any evidence to support his *assertion*?
   - A. court
   - B. judge
   - C. claim

2. Social media sites are perfect *outlets* for nature photographers to share their work.
   - A. channels
   - B. studios
   - C. supporters

3. Riding in small, crowded elevators gives some people *anxiety*.
   - A. nervousness
   - B. inconvenience
   - C. restrictions

4. The airline has strict carry-on limits, but they make an *exception* for parents traveling with young children.
   - A. explanation
   - B. allowance
   - C. suspicion

5. It's *crucial* that we leave enough time at the end of the presentation for a question-and-answer session.
   - A. polite
   - B. important
   - C. optional

B **Complete each sentence below with one of these words or phrases. Remember to use the correct word form.**

| threshold | vie for | cognitive | ubiquitous | at one's fingertips |

1. Squirrels are _____ in this park. It feels like they're in every tree.

2. Thanks to smartphones, stock traders have the latest market and company information _____.

3. Children enrolled in the academy no longer qualify for reduced tuition once their parents pass a certain income _____.

4. Fifty-five applicants are _____ admission to the elite program.

5. The patient is 80 years old, so it's natural that he is exhibiting some memory loss and other signs of _____ decline.

C **Choose the correct form of the words in parentheses.**

1. The (diligent / diligently) lab technician checked her results three times.

2. Watching TV as you fall asleep (interference / interferes) with sleep patterns.

3. One way to develop (tolerant / tolerance) for different ideas is to try to see things from another person's point of view.

4. Good emergency planning was credited with (mitigates / mitigating) the fire's impact.

5. An (enabled / enabler) is someone who encourages a certain type of behavior.

Focus on Language

Word Parts

Study the word parts in the chart below. Then read the pairs of sentences that follow. Decide if the second sentence is true or false.

Word Part	Meaning	Examples
ad-	towards	adversity, adept
-mod-	manner; method	modal, immodest
-scape	the view of a place or concept	moonscape, dreamscape

1. The district's row of skyscrapers is a distinct feature of the cityscape.
   The area's tall buildings are a minor part of the city's view. (True / False)

2. Children tend to be skillful at adapting to new technology like mobile devices.
   Kids are good at learning to use new devices. (True / False)

3. You can modify the safety settings to restrict the websites that may be visited.
   Adjusting the settings places limits on Internet use. (True / False)

Grammar & Usage   *Had better & Better off*

Better is used in several ways to suggest that a certain action is preferable. One common usage is with the structure "had better + original verb." Another is with the structure "better off + v-ing."

Ex: We <u>had better stay</u> with the original plan.

Ex: Jonathan is <u>better off finishing</u> his graduate studies before getting a job.

Put the words in the correct sentence order.

1. (cracked screen / getting the / repaired / is better off / George).

   _____

2. (charge your / long bus ride / You had / phone before the / better).

   _____

3. (old TV / replacing / better off / Are we / the)?

   _____

Listening Listen to the conversation. Then answer these questions.

Track 34

1. (   ) Who is Mike?
   - (A) Linda's boyfriend
   - (B) The man and woman's son
   - (C) Cheryl's school friend
   - (D) A visiting neighbor

2. (   ) How do the man and woman feel about installing security software?
   - (A) They feel the same way about it.
   - (B) They agree with Cheryl's position.
   - (C) They think it's too expensive.
   - (D) They believe it can build trust.

3. (   ) What does the man suggest?
   - (A) Eating dinner early
   - (B) Buying a new cell phone
   - (C) Discussing things with Mike
   - (D) Going out this evening

Reading Fill in each blank with a word or phrase from each group below.

Many parents feel giving their toddlers early access to electronic media will give them a leg up in a competitive world. However, despite the presence of more than 80,000 educational apps on the market, there is (1) research supporting their effectiveness. How, then, should young kids spend their time? Ironically, one of the best ways to plan out playtime is to not plan it at all. "Unstructured" play is (2) to stimulate young kids' creativity and problem-solving skills. Classic toys like sets of blocks have endless possibilities, allowing kids to build houses, roads, and other structures. Even better, when parents talk to toddlers about their creations, it (3) communication and vocabulary skills.

1. (   )
   - (A) few
   - (B) little
   - (C) many
   - (D) lot

2. (   )
   - (A) highly encouraged
   - (B) high encouragement
   - (C) higher encouraging
   - (D) highest to encourage

3. (   )
   - (A) replies
   - (B) displaces
   - (C) improves
   - (D) imagines

12 Wealth and Giving

The World of the Super Rich

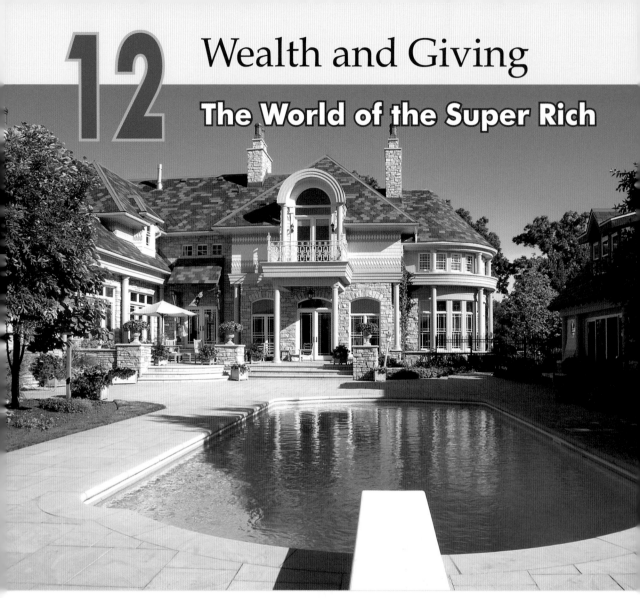

Worldwide, there are around 200,000 super-rich people worth $30 million or more. They are able to live their lives any way they want. Their spending choices take many forms, and some choose to give away most of their money.

Pre-Reading Questions Discuss these questions in pairs.

1. How would you spend your money if you were extremely rich?

2. Do wealthy people have a responsibility to donate to charity?

3. What problems, if any, do you think rich people have?

Vocabulary Warm-up Track 35

A Read and listen to this list of the unit's target vocabulary. Write the letter of the target word or phrase next to the correct definition.

a. alleviate	f. concierge	k. inheritance
b. appeal (n)	g. consumption	l. lavish
c. asset	h. cunning	m. make inroads
d. broker (v)	i. exist	n. mansion
e. charity	j. frugal	o. yacht

___ 1. very large house

___ 2. help someone sell or arrange something

___ 3. attraction; interest

___ 4. very clever

___ 5. careful about spending money

___ 6. group that performs a public service, helps those in need, etc.

___ 7. money or goods received from someone who has died

___ 8. make better; lessen an impact

___ 9. recreational boat (often with sleeping quarters, cooking facilities, etc.)

___ 10. luxurious

B Complete each sentence with the correct word or phrase from the list above. Remember to use the correct word form.

1. Let's ask the hotel _____ to arrange a tour of Buenos Aires.

2. Stocks are a type of _____ that investors tend to hold for years before selling.

3. If we want to _____ in the market, we need to spend more on advertising. Otherwise, our position won't improve.

4. My neighbors reduced their energy _____ by 8% by replacing their old refrigerator and air conditioner.

5. Relatively few large animals _____ in the region, probably due to the limited fresh water supply.

Reading Passage Track 36

Like the kings and queens of the ancient world, there **exists** a class of people in modern times with nearly unimaginable wealth. These brilliant entrepreneurs and **cunning** businesspeople have built fortunes that allow them to buy whatever they want and, should they choose, perform tremendous charitable

5 deeds. The world of the super rich is complex. Many wealthy people buy palatial **mansions** and exquisite jewels; some live frugally and work full-time; others devote their lives to philanthropic efforts; and some do a little bit of everything.

Over the last 30 years, there has been a marked concentration of wealth in

10 a small number of hands. In 2018, the richest 0.8% of the world's population controlled 44.8% of its wealth. That year, there were around 200,000 super-rich people with **assets** of at least $30 million, including 2,229 billionaires. North America, Europe, and Asia are home to two-thirds of the super wealthy. Most made their money in fields like finance, fashion, real estate, and manufacturing,

15 while 30% received some or all of their fortunes from **inheritances**.

With vast resources at one's disposal, conspicuous **consumption** is on full display. Real estate has long been a favored sector. Estates may include everything from tennis courts to beaches, ski lifts,

20 and even private power plants. In 2010, India's richest person spent an estimated $1-$2 billion constructing a multi-story mansion in Mumbai. Another gorgeous estate, called Villa Leopolda, is in Côte d'Azur, France. Its value is $750 million. Then

Yachts are not only status symbols, but they can be used to travel long distances in comfort.

25 there are homes for use on the open sea – stunning super **yachts** whose size and design are limited only by one's imagination. The most **lavish** of these, named the History Supreme, is covered with gold and worth $4.8 billion.

Other interests and hobbies command prices that must be seen to be

30 believed. Desired objects include artworks, coins, jewelry, and cars. 2018 was an especially striking year for extravagant spending. A painting by David Hockney sold for $90.3 million; a 1962 Ferrari went for $48 million; and a 19-carat pink diamond was purchased for $50 million. As an encapsulation of this level of spending, consider the sale of 1,500 items from the Rockefeller

35 Estate, **brokered** by famed auction house Christie's. Once the final gavel fell, the items totaled $833 million.

Interestingly, for those who have it all, the pursuit of material objects can lose its **appeal**. There is a strong demand among the super rich for unforgettable adventures. Billionaire Richard Branson became famous for his record-setting
40 balloon trips. Others have traveled beneath the oceans in private submarines. And some have paid a small fortune to fly to the International Space Station. Back on Earth, there are specialized **concierge** services that can arrange nearly any experience you want.

And yet, not all wealthy people are lavish spenders. Some are quite **frugal**.
45 Facebook founder Mark Zuckerberg famously wears jeans and tennis shoes instead of fancy suits. Microsoft founder Bill Gates uses a $10 watch. And Mexican billionaire Carlos Slim Helú drives himself around rather than rely on a chauffeur. Leading by example, these billionaires want their children to learn the value of hard work and personal accomplishment.

50 In fact, a growing number of wealthy individuals, rather than leave everything to their children, are donating vast sums to charitable causes. By 2019, 190 super-wealthy people had signed the Giving Pledge, promising to donate at least 50% of their assets to **charity**. Philanthropic efforts have helped non-profit organizations **make inroads** in vaccinating children, **alleviating**
55 poverty, and protecting the environment. For example, the Tompkins Conservation, established by the family that founded Esprit and The North Face, has bought and preserved millions of acres of land in Argentina and Chile. Other individuals are leading similar efforts in Scotland, South Africa, and elsewhere, with much of the land eventually being integrated into
60 national park systems.

As fascinating as the lives of the super rich are, it's worth remembering that deep down, they are people like the rest of us. Loneliness and anxiety are common since wealthy people have to be cautious about who they can trust, including careful consideration of relatives, friends, and financial advisors.
65 At the same time, great wealth has the potential to not only provide an extraordinary existence for oneself and one's family, but also to change the world on an unprecedented scale.

---

[2] unimaginable – hard to believe or imagine   [2] entrepreneur – business founder or inventor
[6] palatial – gigantic; as big as a palace   [6] exquisite – beautiful and luxurious
[7] philanthropic – related to donating time and money to good causes   [9] marked – strong; clear
[16] conspicuous – very obvious   [25] stunning – beautiful; shocking   [29] command – be valued at; cost   [31] extravagant – bold and often excessive   [33] encapsulation – representation
[35] gavel – hammer-like item that is struck on a hard surface to make noise   [48] chauffeur – driver
[52] pledge – promise   [67] unprecedented – never-before-seen

Choose the best answer to each question.

.... Main Idea

1. (   ) What is the main idea of the reading?
    A: Great wealth has many uses, including personal enjoyment and charity.
    B. Real estate is an excellent investment, regardless of your level of wealth.
    C. Up to $2 billion was spent on the construction of a mansion in India.
    D. Of the 200,000 people with $30 million, there are only 2,229 billionaires.

.... Detail

2. (   ) What is the value of the world's most luxurious yacht?
    A. $90.3 million   B. $833 million
    C. $1.5 billion   D. $4.8 billion

.... Vocabulary

3. (   ) In line 16, what does "at one's disposal" mean?
    A. purchased   B. discarded
    C. available   D. convincing

.... Analysis

4. (   ) What does the article imply about Richard Branson's balloon trips?
    A. Balloon rides are just another type of conspicuous consumption.
    B. Similar record-setting trips have been attempted by other billionaires.
    C. Such adventures are more exciting than stays at a space station.
    D. They exemplify the way wealthy people pursue memorable experiences.

5. (   ) What is suggested about philanthropic efforts by the super wealthy?
    A. Nearly half of the world's billionaires have signed the Giving Pledge.
    B. They may involve cooperating with a country's national services.
    C. Environmental causes receive more donations than other movements.
    D. The children of the super wealthy oversee most charitable efforts.

Short Answers Write a full-sentence answer to each question.

1. In 2018, how many super-rich people were there worldwide?

   _____

2. What do specialized concierge services do for wealthy people?

   _____

3. How has the Tompkins Conservation helped protect the environment?

   _____

Vocabulary Building

A Choose the answer that is a synonym for the word or phrase in italics.

1. Buying the fast-growing competitor was a *cunning* move by the electronics giant.
   A. intelligent　　　　B. costly　　　　C. digital

2. The *mansion* is so large that it has three parking garages.
   A. harbor　　　　B. vehicle　　　　C. estate

3. The corporate headquarters is the insurance company's most substantial *asset*.
   A. assumption　　　　B. possession　　　　C. contribution

4. Since the painting is valuable, the family is using an art gallery to *broker* the sale.
   A. restore　　　　B. appraise　　　　C. handle

5. It may take us years to *make inroads* in Brazil because of the market's complexity.
   A. evaluate　　　　B. expand　　　　C. justify

B Complete each sentence below with one of these words. Remember to use the correct word form.

inheritance	charity	yacht	concierge	alleviate

1. The _____ secured us tickets for the hottest new musical, so I gave him a generous tip.

2. This _____ will sail to Cannes, France, on the eve of the film festival.

3. Each of the billionaire's children received a(n) _____ of hundreds of millions of dollars.

4. The heiress supports two _____ which rescue abused animals.

5. To _____ the pressure of running a multinational corporation, the CEO takes regular vacations to the Caribbean.

C Choose the correct form of the words in parentheses.

1. Meredith is eager for a new direction in life since she doesn't want her (exist / existence) to be all about working and paying bills.

2. Although known for his (frugality / frugally) when it comes to clothing, Mark Zuckerberg has an impressive real estate portfolio.

3. The hotel is decorated so (lavishness / lavishly) that it has been featured in leading travel magazines.

4. The cell phone plant (consuming / consumes) more energy than any other factory in the area.

5. We need to (appeal / appealing) to young shoppers while retaining our core base.

Focus on Language

Word Parts

Study the word parts in the chart below. Then read the pairs of sentences that follow. Decide if the second sentence is true or false.

Word Part	Meaning	Examples
pur-	before; favoring	pursue, purpose
-phil-	love	philanthropist, bibliophile
-plex	having multiple parts	duplex, perplex

1. The metroplex is so important to the region that a new airport was built to serve its residents and businesses.

   The area's people and companies are concentrated in just one city. (True / False)

2. Since Jennifer is an audiophile, we should get her the best headphones on the market.

   Jennifer is passionate about the sound quality of her music. (True / False)

3. The Code of Ur-Nammu is purported to be the world's oldest legal code.

   The claim is that no other law codes are as old. (True / False)

Grammar & Usage   *Rather & Rather than*

> *Rather* is used before an adjective or other word to mean "quite" or to express a preference. *Rather* can also present multiple options. *Rather than* indicates a choice. It can also mean "instead of."
>
> Ex: That was a <u>rather</u> stunning vocal performance.
>
> Ex: Would you <u>rather</u> stay home or take a walk?
>
> Ex: <u>Rather than</u> eat there again, I'd prefer a Greek restaurant.

Put the words in the correct sentence order.

1. (a rather / Gandhi's life / interesting movie / It was / about).

   _____

2. (invest in / real estate / Would you / stocks or / rather)?

   _____

3. (the problem, / solve it / worry about / Rather than / let's).

   _____

Listening   Listen to the short talk. Then answer these questions.

Track 37

1. (   ) What is the purpose of the talk?
   - (A) To provide career advice
   - (B) To promote a new book
   - (C) To announce a seminar
   - (D) To advertise a future show

2. (   ) What does *The Thin Green Line* say about wealthy people?
   - (A) They typically cook at home.
   - (B) They prefer expensive cars.
   - (C) They tend to be avid readers.
   - (D) They are fans of *Money Talk*.

3. (   ) What do we learn about the special guest?
   - (A) He has been on the program before.
   - (B) He is the author of several books.
   - (C) He hopes to be an investor someday.
   - (D) He made his fortune in real estate.

Reading   Fill in each blank with a word or phrase from each group below.

Income inequality is receiving significant coverage in both the press and scholarly research. That's not surprising, considering the world's richest 256,000 people were worth a staggering $31.5 trillion in 2018. That's more than the (1) GDPs of most of the world's top 10 economies. In countries like the US, corporate profits have soared, while wages have struggled to keep pace.

And yet, income inequality is a complicated issue (2) must be looked at on a country-by-country basis. Inequality has worsened since 1990 in many of the world's largest economies, including the US, China, and India. In the developing world, however, the situation has improved. Countries like Senegal, Algeria, and Mali have experienced a more (3) distribution of wealth since 1990.

1. (   )   (A) combining   (B) combined
                 (C) to combine   (D) combines

2. (   )   (A) which   (B) where
                 (C) when   (D) what

3. (   )   (A) calculable   (B) deniable
                 (C) inflatable   (D) equitable

13 Animals

The Emotions of Animals

Some long-held beliefs about animals are being reconsidered. Respect for their intelligence is growing, as is the evidence that they experience happiness, jealousy, and other emotions just like people. These findings are impacting the way animals are raised and treated.

Pre-Reading Questions   Discuss these questions in pairs.

1. Have you ever raised a cat, dog, bird, or other pet? If so, what type of animal was it?

2. Have you ever seen an animal display happiness, sadness, or another emotion? If so, describe what you saw.

3. In your opinion, are humans and animals completely different, or do they have anything in common?

Vocabulary Warm-up Track 38

A **Read and listen to this list of the unit's target vocabulary. Write the letter of the target word or phrase next to the correct definition.**

a. alter	f. console	k. mammal
b. assume	g. criteria	l. overwhelming
c. automaton	h. domestic	m. perilous
d. buck a trend	i. facility	n. psychological
e. capable	j. layperson	o. signify

___ 1. able to do something; competent

___ 2. non-expert; common person

___ 3. change; modify

___ 4. non-thinking machine

___ 5. very dangerous

___ 6. go against a popular idea or practice

___ 7. give comfort; make someone feel better

___ 8. extremely powerful; great

___ 9. suppose; believe you know something, even without proof

___ 10. indicate; mean

B **Complete each sentence with the correct word or phrase from the list above. Remember to use the correct word form.**

1. Elephants, the largest of all the land _____, live in close-knit communities.

2. The selection _____ for people wanting to join the Amazon expedition include language skills and physical fitness.

3. Cats and dogs are the most common _____ pets, but animal lovers also raise snakes, pigs, and other creatures.

4. Tigers and monkeys kept by zoos in small cages may suffer from long-term _____ problems, including depression and anti-social behavior.

5. The _____ has the equipment we'll need to heal the injured eagle.

Reading Passage Track 39

In a show of empathy, a humpback whale rescues a seal from a pack of killer whales. In a show of sadness, an elephant grieves over the loss of a child. These are among the many examples of emotional behavior seen in animals. Pet owners have long known that their cats, dogs, and birds are **capable** of joy,
5   sadness, and jealousy. New research is revealing a great range of emotions throughout the animal kingdom – on land, in the air, and in the ocean.

Emotions are complex phenomena with three components: behavioral (the outward expression that others see), physiological (the way one's body reacts), and **psychological** (one's thoughts and reflections). There are evolutionary
10   advantages to responding emotionally to situations. By being fearful and remembering painful experiences, you learn to avoid harmful encounters. By being jealous, you compete for resources, improving your chances to eat and procreate. Without these abilities, surviving in a **perilous** world would be difficult.

15   However, for most of human history, it has been widely **assumed** that only people are capable of complex reasoning and emotions. Animals were thought to be governed by rigid, instinctive behavior. In 1872, Charles Darwin **bucked**
20   **the trend** by writing about the way animals' expressions revealed their inner feelings. His work was criticized for many years, and scientists and **laypeople** continued to classify animal behavior

Primates have especially complex emotional lives and social structures.

differently from that of humans. These distinctions were even codified
25   linguistically. For instance, while humans "loved" one another, animals were said to "form pair bonds." Such classifications diminished the depth of animals' feelings and the importance of their inner lives.

The tide started to turn when researchers examined whether animals feel pain the way people do. The evidence was **overwhelming**. Just like humans, other
30   **mammals** – and even fish – meet all the **criteria** for feeling pain. They possess nociceptors, which send signals to the brain **signifying** that part of the body is in distress. Their behavior changes dramatically when they are hurt. Also, administering pain killers relieves the suffering. These findings have impacted the way animals are treated by businesses, zoos, and medical research **facilities**.

35   Other studies have provided evidence that animals experience emotions in similar ways to people. Ravens have been observed **consoling** individuals

who lost a conflict. After the death of an infant, baboons have elevated levels of glucocorticoid hormones, which are also associated with grief in humans. And brain scans are finally allowing us to observe high-level neurological
40 functions. Researchers at the Hungarian Academy of Sciences trained dogs to sit still during an MRI scan. The scientists discovered that when dogs hear sounds like laughter or crying, their brains light up in an area near the primary auditory cortex, just like a person's brain.

Such findings have practical implications. For example, horses are known to
45 suffer from depression when exposed to prolonged stressful conditions. The behavior is observable from horses' body language, and it is measurable since lower cortisol levels in the blood may indicate a depressed state. With this knowledge, farmers and breeders can **alter** their treatment of horses to improve their living conditions. Evidence also shows that fish feel not only pain but also
50 happiness, anger, and excitement. Now that we know they are not mindless **automatons**, adjustments can be made to the way they are captured and bred.

Steps have been taken to acknowledge these findings at high governmental and academic levels. In 1997, the European Union passed the Amsterdam Treaty, which recognized that animals have emotions. Going a step further, in
55 2012 an international group of scientists, including Stephen Hawking, signed the Cambridge Declaration of Consciousness. It states that mammals, birds, octopuses, and other animals are, like people, conscious. Recognizing that animals are sentient respects their individuality, and it acknowledges that they value their lives and those of their loved ones.

60 Animals enrich our lives in many ways. A study of dog owners showed that when distraught, pet owners are more likely to seek comfort from their dogs than from friends or relatives. The UK group Pets As Therapy has 5,000 dogs which brighten the lives of 130,000 people weekly in hospitals, nursing homes, and elsewhere. We derive comfort and companionship from these interactions.
65 It's validating to know that animals, both **domestic** and wild, also experience emotions as part of their complex and fascinating lives.

---

[7] phenomena (singular: phenomenon) – happenings; occurrences   [8] physiological – related to the body   [13] procreate – have children   [24] codify – create a system or set of rules for something   [26] pair bond – a couple that mates and stays together
[28] a turning of the tide – a change of direction or fortune   [31] nociceptor – neuron that senses pain and danger   [43] cortex – a part of the brain   [47] cortisol – hormone related to stress
[48] breeder – someone who raises and sells animals   [56] consciousness – awareness of who you are   [58] sentient – alive, conscious, and feeling   [61] distraught – sad or bothered
[64] derive – get; receive   [65] validating – reassuring; confirming

Choose the best answer to each question.

.... **Main Idea**

1. (   ) What is the main idea of the reading?
   A. Empathy, sadness, and other emotions make life more meaningful.
   B. Animals must control their emotions in order to survive.
   C. Certain experiences trigger strong emotional reactions.
   D. Recent findings confirm the richness of animals' emotional lives.

.... **Detail**

2. (   ) Which of the following would indicate that fish feel physical pain?
   A. Lower amounts of cortisol
   B. Higher-than-normal glucocorticoid levels
   C. The presence of nociceptors
   D. Activity in the primary auditory cortex

.... **Vocabulary**

3. (   ) In line 1, what does "pack" mean?
   A. sack   B. group
   C. bundle   D. leader

.... **Analysis**

4. (   ) Which aspect of animal emotions did Charles Darwin write about in 1872?
   A. Behavioral   B. Physiological
   C. Psychological   D. All of the above

5. (   ) Which of these statements would the signers of the Cambridge Declaration of Consciousness likely agree with?
   A. Within an animal species, all its members have identical personalities.
   B. Apes and ravens are conscious, but smaller mammals probably aren't.
   C. Animals are aware of who they are, and they are unique individuals.
   D. We should use different terms to discuss animal and human emotions.

Short Answers **Write a full-sentence answer to each question.**

1. What are the three types of emotional components?

   _____

2. What evidence exists that baboons experience grief similarly to the way people do?

   _____

3. What are four sensations that fish feel?

   _____

Vocabulary Building

A Choose the answer that is a synonym for the word or phrase in italics.

1. Ravens meet the *criteria* for being considered highly intelligent.
   A. requirements   B. experiments   C. comparisons

2. Determining an animal's *psychological* state is often difficult.
   A. mental   B. linguistic   C. aggressive

3. The *facility* housing the camping gear is near the south gate.
   A. seller   B. equipment   C. building

4. Although donations have been declining, we're hoping to *buck the trend* with this summer's fund-raising drive.
   A. reverse the norm   B. accept the challenge   C. decrease the output

5. The long drought compelled local wildlife to *alter* their feeding routines.
   A. restore   B. reduce   C. revise

B Complete each sentence below with one of these words. Remember to use the correct word form.

mammal   layperson   automaton   console   overwhelming

1. Much more than a simple _____, the X350 is driven by sophisticated AI with the ability to learn and evolve.

2. The grieving ape was _____ by relatives and other group members.

3. Communication departments prepare charts and presentations so that technical discoveries can be understood by a(n) _____.

4. The movement to expand the nature preserve has received _____ public support.

5. _____ are warm-blooded animals, and most have hair or fur.

C Choose the correct form of the words in parentheses.

1. Once a wild animal is (domestically / domesticated), it may not be able to survive on its own again.

2. Our intern handled the reorganization of the filing system (capably / capability).

3. Does the extra set of paw prints by the lake have any (signifying / significance)?

4. Let's resist making (assumptions / assumes) about the herd's location until the aerial survey is complete.

5. Most of the world's big cat species are (perilously / perilous) close to extinction.

Focus on Language

Word Parts

Study the word parts in the chart below. Then read the pairs of sentences that follow. Decide if the second sentence is true or false.

Word Part	Meaning	Examples
inter-	between	interior, interact
-phys-	nature	metaphysics, physical
-ly	in such a way	hopefully, reportedly

1. Jane Goodall observed the interplay of wild chimpanzees in great detail.

   She saw the way the animals lived together in a natural setting. (True / False)

2. As the biologist watched through binoculars, the bird unexpectedly shared its food with another member of the flock.

   The biologist knew the bird would behave that way. (True / False)

3. The physicality of gorillas, which are able to lift hundreds of kilograms, is impressive.

   Gorillas have natural characteristics which make them very strong. (True / False)

Grammar & Usage   *By + V-ing*

We use this structure to explain how a condition makes an action possible. The condition is contained in a phrase which can come at the beginning or end of the sentence.

Ex: <u>By setting up</u> a hidden camera, we can observe the nest day and night.

Ex: Peacocks attract mates <u>by displaying and shaking</u> their feathers.

Put the words in the correct sentence order.

1. (dolphins' language use, / about their / By studying / social structure / we'll learn more).

   _____

2. (nervous by raising / are happy or / Cats show that they / their tails / or lowering).

   _____

3. (a companion, / the goat / you'll improve / By giving / its mood significantly).

   _____

Listening Listen to the short talk. Then answer these questions.

Track 40

1. (   ) What can be found in the South Wind Nature Preserve?
    - (A) Millions of insect species
    - (B) Thousands of tribespeople
    - (C) Dozens of research teams
    - (D) Hundreds of types of animals

2. (   ) After finishing their field work, how long do grant recipients have before they must publish their findings?
    - (A) 1 week
    - (B) 75 days
    - (C) 9 months
    - (D) 3 years

3. (   ) What information about team members DOES NOT need to be listed by grant applicants?
    - (A) Articles that they've written
    - (B) Field work experience
    - (C) Any donations to South Wind
    - (D) Each member's name

Reading Fill in each blank with a word or phrase from each group below.

Humans are very good at reading emotions on each other's faces. (1   ), we are less adept at discerning what an animal is thinking or feeling. A century after Charles Darwin's groundbreaking work on animal expressions, researchers are revisiting the topic. The hope is that we can codify the meanings behind a narrowed eye, raised eyebrow, or folded ear.

Significant advancements have already been made in (2   ) expressions that reveal when an animal is in pain. The so-called "grimace scale" is remarkably similar among horses, rats, sheep, and other animals. And that's just the beginning. One day, it may be possible to point a phone or other device at an animal and, based on its expression, receive an (3   ) of its emotional state.

1. (   )
    - (A) Therefore
    - (B) Likewise
    - (C) However
    - (D) Instead

2. (   )
    - (A) identify
    - (B) to identify
    - (C) identified
    - (D) identifying

3. (   )
    - (A) indication
    - (B) isolation
    - (C) information
    - (D) irritation

14 Space

Alien Linguistics

Having a conversation with other people can be difficult. Imagine trying to figure out how to speak with an alien race when we aren't even sure how they will communicate. Scientists are searching for alien species and preparing what to do in case we encounter one.

Pre-Reading Questions   Discuss these questions in pairs.

1. If you could send a message to outer space with the hope that it might reach an alien species, what would you say?

2. If we make contact with an alien race, how do you think it will happen? (For example, will we visit them? Will they send us a message?)

3. What may be some obstacles involved with communicating with an alien face-to-face?

Vocabulary Warm-up Track 41

A Read and listen to this list of the unit's target vocabulary. Write the letter of the target word or phrase next to the correct definition.

a. astronomer	f. methodical	k. query
b. component	g. nascent	l. relatively speaking
c. cosmos	h. plausible	m. time interval
d. decipher	i. possess	n. trace one's roots
e. hold out hope	j. presence	o. transmit

___ 1. send out

___ 2. possible; believable

___ 3. length of time between two events

___ 4. decode; figure out

___ 5. own; have

___ 6. believe there is still a chance

___ 7. part of something

___ 8. universe

___ 9. recently begun; fairly new

___ 10. question

B Complete each sentence with the correct word or phrase from the list above. Remember to use the correct word form.

1. _____, this image of the galaxy is excellent. Previous images weren't as detailed.

2. Dr. Simon is a(n) _____ chemist. She carefully does her experiments to ensure the quality of the results.

3. _____ may wait months or years for a chance to use the world's biggest telescopes.

4. The _____ of water on a planet is an indication that it may host life.

5. Modern astronomy _____ to giants of the field like Copernicus, Galileo, and Kepler.

The ongoing search for extraterrestrial life is driven by the question: "Are we alone in the universe?" Alien linguistics, a growing **component** of the effort, explores the way we might communicate with another life form. Will our first contact be a message that we receive? Will it be an alien response
5   to a message that we send out? Or will there be a face-to-face meeting? It's a multidisciplinary field involving **astronomers**, linguists, biologists, and others who are listening to the stars, reaching out to announce our **presence**, and figuring out how to speak with alien species.

At this stage, the **nascent** field of alien linguistics has more questions than
10   answers. One **query** involves the way another species might **transmit** a message across space. For more than half a century, practitioners of SETI (the search for extraterrestrial intelligence) have used radio telescopes to seek out interstellar signals. It's logical to look for radio waves since our planet uses them extensively. Optical telescopes are also pointed skyward in case laser
15   beams are the chosen vehicle of transmission. It's also possible that more exotic channels such as neutrino beams or gravitational waves could be used. The more we learn about the **cosmos**, the more we discover potential avenues of communication.

From time to time, unexplained signals are
20   received, resulting in a flurry of activity. A great deal of excitement has been generated by fast radio bursts (FRBs). They were first detected in 2007 by Professor Duncan Lorimer and David Narkevic, his student. FRBs are incredibly
25   powerful yet brief bursts of energy originating in distant galaxies. FRB 121102 has gained the most interest since it sends out signals of varying intensity at irregular **time intervals**. Astronomers

Besides being used by Frank Drake, the Arecibo radio telescope appeared in the film Contact.

speculate that FRBs could be natural products of neutron stars, supernovas, or
30   black holes. However, some SETI enthusiasts **hold out hope** that they could be generated by an intelligent species.

The counterpart to searching for incoming signals is the creation of our own. The field of METI (messaging extraterrestrial intelligence) **traces its roots** to Frank Drake, who sent a star-bound message in 1974 using the Arecibo
35   radio telescope. METI practitioners, hoping to avoid misunderstandings with alien races, give a great deal of thought to the composition of messages. To

an alien culture, even a simple image of someone reaching out a hand could be misconstrued as a hostile gesture. At the same time, messages in human languages may be impossible to **decipher**. Fortunately, we **possess** two
40   excellent tools which advanced species are likely to understand: mathematics and science. A message containing a basic scientific principle would establish our presence and form the basis of a dialogue.

What star systems, then, should we reach out to? The best candidates are those containing exoplanets in the star's "habitable zone," meaning their
45   distance from the star provides the greatest likelihood for hosting life. In 2017, a message was sent from Norway to the red dwarf GJ 273, a star 12.5 light years away which is orbited by exoplanet GJ 273b. The message started with a series of prime numbers to establish its artificial nature. It also contained short musical compositions. **Relatively speaking**, GJ 273b is nearby, yet if we
50   receive a response, it won't arrive for at least 25 years.

Another component of alien linguistics considers how a face-to-face meeting with an extraterrestrial might unfold. As humans, we take for granted the universality of spoken language. However, it is **plausible** that another species could have a language based on color, magnetic pulses, or logograms. The
55   latter possibility was explored in the movie *Arrival*, in which alien ships flew to Earth and made contact with humans. The heroine was a linguist who applied a **methodical** approach to learning the aliens' language.

Researchers admit the likelihood of such an encounter is small. It's more widely thought that first contact, should it occur, will be in the form of a
60   message that we acquire. Such a scenario was covered in Carl Sagan's science fiction novel *Contact*, which later became a movie. Many of the characters mirrored the efforts of real-world SETI and METI practitioners. Science, teamwork, and sheer ingenuity were used to detect and decode the alien message. For now, instances of interstellar communication exist only in fiction.
65   Yet scientists want to be prepared should we make contact. If we do, it will profoundly impact how we see our place in the universe.

---

[1] extraterrestrial – alien   [6] multidisciplinary – involving more than one field of study
[11] practitioner – someone who studies and practices an activity   [13] interstellar – between stars
[15] vehicle – method; channel   [16] neutrino – a type of subatomic particle   [20] flurry – rush
[38] misconstrue – mistake   [44] exoplanet – planet outside our solar system   [52] unfold – happen
[53] universality – happening everywhere   [54] logogram – a written character that represents a word (ex: Chinese characters)   [62] mirror – be the same   [63] sheer – pure; total
[63] ingenuity – cleverness

.... **Main Idea**

1. (   ) What is the main idea of the reading?
   A. Astronomers, linguists, and biologists like cooperating on difficult tasks.
   B. Scientists are working hard to contact and communicate with aliens.
   C. Carl Sagan had a major impact on SETI and METI's development.
   D. Alien linguists are creating a communication method based on colors.

.... **Detail**

2. (   ) Which possible means of sending an intergalactic signal is NOT discussed?
   A. Zeta rays   B. Radio waves
   C. Gravitational waves   D. Laser beams

.... **Vocabulary**

3. (   ) In line 41, what does "principle" mean?
   A. leading person   B. basic law
   C. school administrator   D. scientific method

.... **Analysis**

4. (   ) Why is a space-bound message including only prime numbers preferable to one containing a video of a person holding something in the air?
   A. Messages containing videos are too large to transmit into space.
   B. We can't agree which country's citizen should be shown.
   C. The message with the numbers is less likely to be misunderstood.
   D. The first message would travel much faster than the second one.

5. (   ) What can we infer about messages sent into space from Earth?
   A. Exoplanets orbiting red dwarf stars are the only ones we should contact.
   B. Northern European transmission sites work best because of the climate.
   C. Receiving a response, even from nearby exoplanets, will take decades.
   D. We should focus on sending messages to the most active FRB sources.

Short Answers   Write a full-sentence answer to each question.

1. What are fast radio bursts?

   _____

2. Besides spoken words, what else might form the basis of an alien language?

   _____

3. If we make contact with an alien race, how is it most widely expected to occur?

   _____

Vocabulary Building

A **Choose the answer that is a synonym for the word or phrase in italics.**

1. The *nascent* field of exo-meteorology involves the study of other planets' weather.
   A. young   B. galactic   C. complex

2. *Relatively speaking*, the Earth is a small planet in our solar system.
   A. Fortunately   B. Realistically   C. Comparatively

3. The *presence* of liquid water beneath the surface of Mars is an exciting possibility.
   A. existence   B. speculation   C. purpose

4. The payload, guidance, and propulsion systems are three of the rocket's main *components*.
   A. costs   B. parts   C. tasks

5. Our school's science fair *traces its roots* to a small competition held in 1967.
   A. chooses its winners   B. charts its history   C. publishes its mission

B **Complete each sentence below with one of these words or phrases. Remember to use the correct word form.**

> query   astronomer   hold out hope   cosmos   time interval

1. There may be billions of exoplanets scattered throughout the

   _____.

2. We are _____ that Dr. Yoshida will join our fact-finding mission.

3. The random _____ between radiation bursts coming from FRB 121102 make it hard to know when the next one will occur.

4. In response to your _____, yes, the lecture will be shown online.

5. When studying the stars, _____ use physics, mathematics, and other tools to make sense of their findings.

C **Choose the correct form of the words in parentheses.**

1. The (possess / possession) of sophisticated labs and equipment is one reason MIT is a leading engineering school.

2. Scientists question the (plausible / plausibility) of every new theory.

3. The professor's assistant is (methodical / methodically) checking the test results now.

4. A frequency of 2380 MHz was used to (transmit / transmission) Dr. Drake's 1974 message.

5. (Decipher / Deciphering) this much data will take a powerful computer system.

Focus on Language

Word Parts

Study the word parts in the chart below. Then read the pairs of sentences that follow. Decide if the second sentence is true or false.

Word Part	Meaning	Examples
extra-	beyond	extraordinary, extraneous
-terr-	earth; land	territorial, terrestrial
-ics	a field of study	economics, physics

1. Everyone in the sports therapy department is an expert in biomechanics.
   They have all studied the mechanical functions of the human body. (True / False)

2. The talk show guest claims to be a mind reader with extrasensory perception.
   The guest says he has skills that anyone with typical senses has. (True / False)

3. The terrain up ahead is uneven, so let's proceed with caution.
   They are about to arrive at a flat and unchanging area. (True / False)

Grammar & Usage   *The Future Conditional*

The future conditional states what will or won't happen in the future, based on a stated reason. It contains a cause (an adverb clause starting with "if") and a result (an independent clause containing "will" or "won't").

Ex: <u>If</u> the weather stays like this, the eclipse <u>won't</u> be viewable.

Ex: We <u>will</u> be able to increase the instrument's range <u>if</u> we recalibrate it.

Put the words in the correct sentence order.

1. (double check / If we send / they will / the institute our data, / our calculations).

   _____

2. (canceled / the robot race / stay this low, / will be / If registration numbers).

   _____

3. (won't receive / if they aren't / Alien species / technologically advanced / the message).

   _____

Listening Listen to the conversation. Then answer these questions.

Track 43

1. (   ) What do we learn about the man?
   (A) He has read a lot about astronomy.
   (B) He works as a satellite engineer.
   (C) He can fix radios and other equipment.
   (D) He has already found an alien signal.

2. (   ) How many hours a day does the man scan the sky?
   (A) One   (B) Two
   (C) Three   (D) Four

3. (   ) How does the woman feel about amateur astronomers?
   (A) Doubtful   (B) Supportive
   (C) Jealous   (D) Concerned

Reading Read this passage. Then answer the questions below.

The nature of intelligence, both on our planet and others, is of considerable interest to the scientific community. If we are to communicate with an alien species, we must first understand the parameters of what it means to think. Dr. Marianne Walker is a pre-eminent expert in the field, and next week she will visit our university to tell us about her work.

An award-winning marine biologist, Dr. Walker focuses on non-human intelligence. Her research on cephalopods – in particular the thriving octopus community of Jervis Bay, Australia – has broadened our understanding of how other species think, behave, and interact with one another. After her talk, there will be a 20-minute question-and-answer session, so feel free to prepare any questions you have about cephalopods or alien communication. All students are welcome to attend Dr. Walker's lecture.

1. (   ) What is the purpose of this passage?
   (A) To challenge a theory   (B) To discuss an award
   (C) To describe a project   (D) To announce a lecture

2. (   ) What aspect of Dr. Walker's career is NOT discussed?
   (A) Her current teaching position (B) Her past research projects
   (C) Her academic area of focus   (D) Her species of interest

3. (   ) What are students asked to do?
   (A) Come prepared with questions
   (B) Contribute to Dr. Walker's research
   (C) Join an expedition to Jervis Bay
   (D) Prepare a short response paper

15 The Future

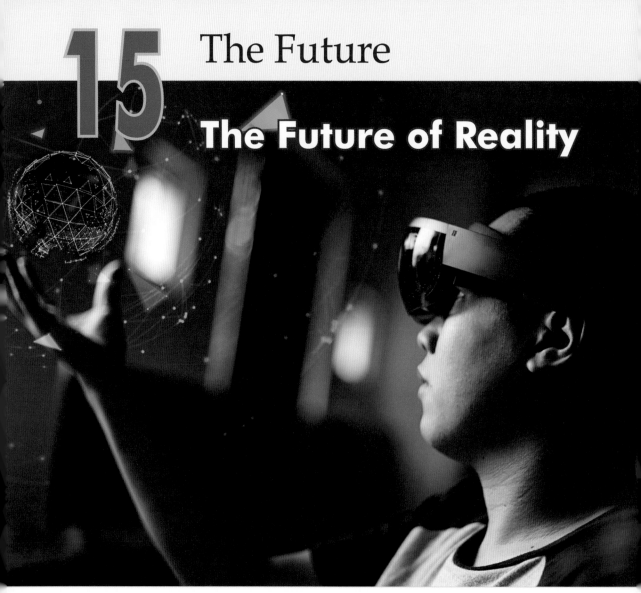

The Future of Reality

Modern technology makes it easy to fabricate photos and videos of nearly anything or anybody. At the same time, we are growing accustomed to seeing and speaking with AI-powered bots. These changes are impacting traditional notions of truth and reality.

Pre-Reading Questions Discuss these questions in pairs.

1. Have you ever received a "robocall" – that is, a phone call generated by an automated computer system? If so, do you remember what it was for?

2. Intelligent digital assistants are becoming popular. How do you feel about having conversations with machines?

3. A growing number of fake videos are being made, making it look like people said and did things they never did. Should we be worried? Why or why not?

Vocabulary Warm-up Track 44

A Read and listen to this list of the unit's target vocabulary. Write the letter of the target word or phrase next to the correct definition.

a. apt	f. distinguish	k. pit against
b. benign	g. imitate	l. probability
c. cat and mouse game	h. intonation	m. proliferate
d. counter-measure	i. likeness	n. sensory
e. defraud	j. nuisance	o. veracity

___ 1. harmless; kind

___ 2. a bother; something troublesome

___ 3. truthfulness

___ 4. likelihood

___ 5. cheat; fool and steal from

___ 6. appropriate

___ 7. spread; multiply

___ 8. try to be like someone or something; copy

___ 9. tell apart; note the difference between things

___ 10. set in opposition to

B Complete each sentence with the correct word or phrase from the list above. Remember to use the correct word form.

1. With its flashing lights and loud noises, the children's toy has been criticized as a(n) _____ overload.

2. Improving the drainage system is one _____ being considered to deal with the flooding issue.

3. When I called Kylie, she said she was fine, but I could tell from her _____ that she was feeling stressed.

4. The search for the fugitive was a(n) _____. Whenever authorities closed in on his position, he changed locations.

5. Well done! The drawing is an amazing _____ of your cousin.

Reading Passage Track 45

"What you see is what you get" is one of the many popular sayings equating **sensory** experience with truth. However, in today's high-tech world, a more **apt** saying may be: "You can't trust your own eyes." Artificial Intelligence (AI) systems are not only **imitating** people's voices and **likenesses**, but they are
5   creating entirely new computer-generated humans. With the potential for both positive and negative applications, such advances may soon require us to question whether every photo, video, and phone call is real, even if it's from someone we know.

As the Internet has grown, we have become familiar with fake messages.
10   Though they appear to originate from legitimate sources, these "spoof" e-mails are designed to steal passwords or otherwise **defraud** recipients. Because such scams are common, Internet users have learned to question the **veracity** of messages. Likewise, spoof phone calls and robocalls are a growing **nuisance**, particularly since the scammer can make the call look like
15   it's coming from a friend or relative. Telecommunications firms are racing to devise effective **counter-measures** to protect the public.

Other uses of advanced technology to mimic people are more **benign**, such as the use of conversational AI systems to run customer call
20   centers. What's more, Google has an interactive bot called Duplex which can help someone make dinner reservations and other appointments. Its **intonation** and speech patterns sound just like a person's. Another company, Lyrebird,
25   has software that imitates voices with proven effectiveness. After receiving an hour of training from a reporter, the bot placed a phone call to his mother, who believed she was speaking with her son.

Digital assistants are increasingly common in homes and offices.

It appears the bots are here to stay. With the popularity of digital assistants
30   like Apple's Siri and Amazon's Alexa, consumers are becoming comfortable speaking with artificial companions, to the point of asking them for relationship advice. In this field, innovative firms continue to stretch our concepts of reality. Magic Leap's digital assistant Mica is an augmented reality 3D avatar that is seen by wearing special glasses. Mica has human-like
35   expressions in addition to powerful communication skills. Mica and other Internet-connected bots will make life easier while redefining our concepts of friendship and identity.

At least with these assistants, we know our interlocutors are artificial. "Deepfakes," ultra-realistic audio and video files made by computers, will
40 strongly test our ability to trust our senses. The leading technology behind deepfakes are generative adversarial networks (GANs), invented by Ian Goodfellow in 2014. The technique involves two AI neural networks **pitted against** each other. The first network, the "generator," starts by creating something like a video of a person talking. The second network, the
45 "discriminator," decides the **probability** that the material is fake. In response, the generator revises the content, and they go back and forth until the discriminator can no longer **distinguish** between what is real and fake. The finished product is often compellingly realistic.

Such mind-bending technology is already widely accessible. For example,
50 Nvidia, a company specializing in computer graphics, has software called StyleGAN which allows anyone to set up a GAN to generate people, animals, buildings, or just about anything you can think of. GANs have constructive uses in physics, medicine, art, and entertainment. Conversely, they can be used to make it seem like a person said something or to create a fake protest,
55 with potentially harmful consequences. The threat posed by deepfakes is considered so significant that DARPA, an arm of the US Department of Defense, is researching ways to identify them. However, it's a **cat and mouse game**. Once a detection method is developed, a GAN can learn to overcome it.

Digitally created humans, landscapes, and other content is **proliferating**
60 in entertainment products, augmented reality applications, virtual reality programs, and social media platforms. We're close to the point where we can't easily ascertain if something is real, and that has serious implications for our collective notions of truth. Some experts believe we need a caller authentication system for phone calls and a tagging system for videos to
65 verify their authenticity. Others say our best defense is to expand public awareness of deepfakes, spoof phone calls, and other fabricated content. That way, we can determine with greater certainty whether our eyes and ears can be believed.

---

[10] spoof – fake   [13] robocall – automated phone call made by a machine
[14] scammer – cheater; criminal who tries to fool people   [21] bot – robot; machine-controlled system
[34] avatar – computer-generated being   [38] interlocutor – person or machine we talk to
[41] generative – creating   [41] adversarial – working against   [42] neural network – self-learning computer system patterned after the human brain   [45] discriminator – that which can tell the difference between things   [48] compellingly – convincingly   [49] mind-bending – affecting what we see and how we think   [56] DARPA – Defense Advanced Research Projects Agency
[62] ascertain – determine   [66] fabricate – make; create

Choose the best answer to each question.

.... **Main Idea**

1. (   ) What is the main idea of the reading?
   A. The impact of digital content and AI systems on the way we see the world is growing.
   B. Spoof e-mails are the primary reason Internet users have learned to be cautious.
   C. Digital assistants are a convenience, but they should not replace human interaction.
   D. The more we understand technology, the better choices we can make about the future.

.... **Detail**

2. (   ) Which company has software that can be trained to mimic someone's voice?
   A. Google   B. Nvidia   C. Lyrebird   D. Magic Leap

.... **Vocabulary**

3. (   ) In line 52, what does "constructive" mean?
   A. scientific   B. beneficial   C. multiple   D. futuristic

.... **Analysis**

4. (   ) What is NOT suggested about digital assistants?
   A. Interacting with all of them requires augmented reality glasses.
   B. Consumers are already having conversations with them.
   C. Some digital assistants can replicate human expressions.
   D. They will make us reconsider traditional ideas of what a friend is.

5. (   ) What does the article imply about GANs?
   A. Since the process is proprietary, the general public is unable to use GANs.
   B. After we learn to identify deepfakes, they will no longer be a concern.
   C. You need one neural network to make deepfake photos, and two for videos.
   D. GANs may have positive applications in both the arts and sciences.

Short Answers Write a full-sentence answer to each question.

1. What is the purpose of spoof e-mails?

_____

2. How can Google's Duplex bot help people?

_____

3. What can people do with StyleGAN?

_____

Vocabulary Building

A Choose the answer that is a synonym for the word in italics.

1. There is a high *probability* that AI-powered sales associates will soon be common.
   A. possibility   B. complication   C. assessment

2. I thought the Halloween costume was a fair *likeness* of Napoleon.
   A. resemblance   B. history   C. festivity

3. For guests, visiting the office building is a *nuisance*, since a guard takes your photo and asks you to fill out a form, and then you are escorted upstairs.
   A. safety   B. judgment   C. annoyance

4. An *apt* response to the security breach would be prohibiting employees from taking computers home.
   A. extreme   B. fearful   C. suitable

5. Mrs. Peterson, who has a *benign* way about her, is eager to help out neighbors.
   A. unique   B. caring   C. popular

B Complete each sentence below with one of these words or phrases. Remember to use the correct word form.

> counter-measure   sensory   distinguish   cat and mouse game   veracity

1. To ensure the _____ of messages and avoid scams, our executives use an encrypted e-mail system.

2. Finding low airfares online is a _____ since airlines may raise prices within hours of posting deals.

3. Walking through a rainforest is an intense _____ experience, featuring an incredible array of sights, sounds, and smells.

4. Being able to _____ between authentic photos and images altered by software like Photoshop takes experience and a good eye.

5. Message alerts, which notify customers when a credit card is used, are among the _____ designed to limit fraudulent card use.

C Choose the correct form of the words in parentheses.

1. How did you determine that the statue is an (imitation / imitating)?

2. In the game, players are (pitted / pitting) against sophisticated AI-powered monsters.

3. The spoof banking website (defrauds / defrauded) 1,300 people before it was shut down.

4. There has been a recent (proliferation / proliferate) of software using GAN techniques.

5. Voice actors need expert powers of (intonate / intonation) to perform their jobs.

Focus on Language

Word Parts

Study the word parts in the chart below. Then read the pairs of sentences that follow. Decide if the second sentence is true or false.

Word Part	Meaning	Examples
ultra-	beyond; extreme	ultraviolet, ultrasonic
-ver-	truth	veritable, unverified
-wise	regarding; in a direction	otherwise, lengthwise

1. The digital forensics team verified the origin and timestamp of the text message.

   The team was able to determine when and from whom the text was sent. *(True / False)*

2. The ultramodern apartment has lighting, security, and climate systems that can be controlled by a mobile device.

   The apartment was patterned after low-tech homes from the 1950s. *(True / False)*

3. To loosen the bolt, rotate it counter-clockwise.

   The bolt should be moved from right to left to loosen it. *(True / False)*

Grammar & Usage   *Particular & Particularly*

Particular is an adjective meaning "specific," "special," or "choosy." *Particularly* is an adverb meaning "especially." It can modify an adjective or appear before an adverb clause for emphasis.

Ex: Jeff is very particular about what he eats.
Ex: I thought it was a particularly interesting lecture.
Ex: Walking through the city is tiring, particularly when it's humid.

Complete each sentence with *particular* or *particularly*.

1. That _____ lens has to be ordered from Germany.

2. We should get to the fairgrounds early, _____ if we want to see the hot air balloons before they launch.

3. I haven't got any _____ ideas in mind. I just thought we'd go to the beach and have fun.

Listening   **Listen to the short talk. Then answer these questions.**

Track 46

1. (   ) What is the purpose of this talk?
   - (A) To sell a cutting-edge product
   - (B) To clarify a misconception
   - (C) To announce a new policy
   - (D) To discuss a public safety issue

2. (   ) What percentage of US phone calls are made by automated systems?
   - (A) 18%   (B) 26%   (C) 30%   (D) 50%

3. (   ) What is implied about software that mimics voices?
   - (A) It makes it easier for criminals to locate victims' phone numbers.
   - (B) It has already made the problem of robocalls more severe.
   - (C) It could be used by a scammer posing as a friend or relative.
   - (D) It may be a useful counter-measure against unwanted phone calls.

Reading   **Fill in each blank with a word from each group below.**

Fabricated videos have been around a long time. In the early 20th century, it took weeks for film footage to travel across the world. That's a lifetime in the field of journalism, so to provide faster reports, news outlets often (1) recreations of major events. These films were added to the newsreels shown at cinemas before a movie began.

For example, to report (2) the massive Japanese earthquake of 1923, an American news outlet used actual photos of the disaster to make 3D miniatures. During filming, they were shaken to simulate a natural disaster, and sulfur and other materials were used to make it appear as if the streets were burning. Though such films were (3) fake, they provided audiences with emotionally stirring accounts.

1. (   )   (A) assumed   (B) produced
               (C) inverted   (D) responded

2. (   )   (A) at   (B) in
               (C) by   (D) on

3. (   )   (A) technically   (B) technician
               (C) technical   (D) technicality

Reading Fusion 3 [B-904]

リーディング フュージョン 3

1　刷	2020 年 1 月 24 日	
3　刷	2023 年 3 月 31 日	
著　者	Andrew E. Bennett	
発行者 発行所	南雲　一範　Kazunori Nagumo 株式会社　南雲堂 〒162-0801　東京都新宿区山吹町 361 NAN'UN-DO CO.,Ltd. 361 Yamabuki-cho, Shinjuku-ku, Tokyo 162-0801, Japan 振替口座：00160-0-46863 TEL：03-3268-2311(代表) ／ FAX：03-3269-2486	
編集者	加藤 敦	
組　版	Office haru	
印刷所	株式会社 木元省美堂	
装　丁	Andrew E. Bennett	
検　印	省略	
コード	ISBN 978-4-523-17904-7	C0082

Printed in Japan

E-mail　nanundo@post.email.ne.jp
URL　　https://www.nanun-do.co.jp/